Accounting: A Very Short Introduction

VERY SHORT INTRODUCTIONS are for anyone wanting a stimulating and accessible way into a new subject. They are written by experts, and have been translated into more than 45 different languages.

The series began in 1995, and now covers a wide variety of topics in every discipline. The VSI library now contains over 500 volumes—a Very Short Introduction to everything from Psychology and Philosophy of Science to American History and Relativity—and continues to grow in every subject area.

Titles in the series include the following:

AFRICAN HISTORY John Parker and
   Richard Rathbone
AGEING Nancy A. Pachana
AGNOSTICISM Robin Le Poidevin
AGRICULTURE Paul Brassley and
   Richard Soffe
ALEXANDER THE GREAT
   Hugh Bowden
ALGEBRA Peter M. Higgins
AMERICAN HISTORY Paul S. Boyer
AMERICAN IMMIGRATION
   David A. Gerber
AMERICAN LEGAL HISTORY
   G. Edward White
AMERICAN POLITICAL
   HISTORY Donald Critchlow
AMERICAN POLITICAL PARTIES
   AND ELECTIONS L. Sandy Maisel
AMERICAN POLITICS
   Richard M. Valelly
THE AMERICAN PRESIDENCY
   Charles O. Jones
AMERICAN SLAVERY
   Heather Andrea Williams
THE AMERICAN WEST Stephen Aron
AMERICAN WOMEN'S HISTORY
   Susan Ware
ANAESTHESIA Aidan O'Donnell
ANARCHISM Colin Ward
ANCIENT EGYPT Ian Shaw
ANCIENT GREECE Paul Cartledge
THE ANCIENT NEAR EAST
   Amanda H. Podany
ANCIENT PHILOSOPHY Julia Annas

ANCIENT WARFARE Harry Sidebottom
ANGLICANISM Mark Chapman
THE ANGLO-SAXON AGE John Blair
ANIMAL BEHAVIOUR
   Tristram D. Wyatt
ANIMAL RIGHTS David DeGrazia
ANXIETY Daniel Freeman and
   Jason Freeman
ARCHAEOLOGY Paul Bahn
ARISTOTLE Jonathan Barnes
ART HISTORY Dana Arnold
ART THEORY Cynthia Freeland
ASTROPHYSICS James Binney
ATHEISM Julian Baggini
THE ATMOSPHERE Paul I. Palmer
AUGUSTINE Henry Chadwick
THE AZTECS David Carrasco
BABYLONIA Trevor Bryce
BACTERIA Sebastian G. B. Amyes
BANKING John Goddard and
   John O. S. Wilson
BARTHES Jonathan Culler
BEAUTY Roger Scruton
THE BIBLE John Riches
BLACK HOLES Katherine Blundell
BLOOD Chris Cooper
THE BODY Chris Shilling
THE BOOK OF MORMON
   Terryl Givens
BORDERS Alexander C. Diener and
   Joshua Hagen
THE BRAIN Michael O'Shea
THE BRICS Andrew F. Cooper
BRITISH POLITICS Anthony Wright

Christopher Nobes

ACCOUNTING

A Very Short Introduction

OXFORD
UNIVERSITY PRESS

OXFORD

UNIVERSITY PRESS

Great Clarendon Street, Oxford, OX2 6DP,
United Kingdom

Oxford University Press is a department of the University of Oxford.
It furthers the University's objective of excellence in research, scholarship,
and education by publishing worldwide. Oxford is a registered trade mark of
Oxford University Press in the UK and in certain other countries

Published in the United States of America by Oxford University Press
198 Madison Avenue, New York, NY 10016, United States of America

British Library Cataloguing in Publication Data

Data available

Library of Congress Control Number: 2013953485

ISBN 978-0-19-968431-1

Printed and bound by
CPI Group (UK) Ltd, Croydon, CR0 4YY

Contents

Preface

Accounting is a very large subject. Accounting records are the
earliest that we have, so accounting is as old as written history.
Managers in corporations and in public sector organizations use
internal accounting reports every day. Published financial
reporting is done several times a year by tens of thousands of
listed companies. The book of rules of International Financial
Reporting Standards is over 3,600 pages long this year; and the
equivalent book of US rules is much longer. So, as for all the
other authors in this series, being 'very short' is a challenge. If
my academic or professional colleagues think that I have
allotted an absurdly short space to their favourite topic (or
omitted it entirely), my excuse is the need for brevity. On the
other hand, my colleagues (especially from the accountancy
profession) might not see any point in the history which I have
included. Fortunately, this book is not intended for my
colleagues, but for the intelligent non-specialist. History, of
course, aids understanding of the present, and it can be
fascinating.

I am grateful for help in making decisions about content to
Andrea Keegan and Emma Ma of Oxford University Press. I also
acknowledge good suggestions for improvement from anonymous
reviewers and from David Alexander (University of Birmingham),

Peter Holgate (PwC), Bob Parker (University of Exeter), and Jim
Rooney (University of Sydney).

Christopher Nobes
Royal Holloway (University of London)
and University of Sydney
July 2013

Accounting

List of illustrations

Accounting

Chapter 1
Introduction

Purpose of the book

If you read the business pages of a newspaper or if you listen to the financial news on the television or radio, you will often hear terms such as 'liability', 'balance sheet', or 'earnings'. These terms turn up in non-financial contexts as well: 'he was more of a liability than an asset'. If you invest in shares, have a building society account, or sit on a committee of a property company which owns your apartment block, you will receive financial statements every year. If you are a manager in a company, a hospital, or a school, you will see accounting information often. This book is designed for you: the intelligent non-specialist.

This book will not turn you into an accountant but it will help you to understand and use accounting information. You will no longer need to feel out-of-depth in conversations that include 'debits', 'pre-tax income', or 'goodwill'. The book will also be a useful introduction to academic or professional study of accounting. The book explains terms when they first appear but, if you get stuck, you can look at the Glossary which explains the key terms.

Importance of accounting

Wherever archaeologists uncover early remains which contain writing or numerals, what they have found are nearly always accounting records. Research shows that the need to keep account was the key driver in the invention of writing and numbers (see Figure 1).

Civilization requires some form of government; which provides roads, defence, order. Government cannot function without tax revenues. Tax cannot work without accounting. So, civilization depends on accounting. Conclusion so far: accounting is important.

In the modern world, prosperity depends on good accounting. The information prepared by accountants is used when making decisions, such as: What price should Tesco or Walmart put on a particular product? Should General Motors build its cars in Michigan or in Malaysia? Should I buy shares in Citibank, HSBC, both, or neither? As a shareholder or a member of a club, should I vote to re-appoint the existing directors?

1. A clay tablet from Sumer, used for numerical records

According to the present rules, how much tax should a company or a person pay this year? What level of dividends should Nokia pay to its shareholders this year?

If these decisions are made badly, the world will be worse off. There will eventually be less money for important things such as hospitals, bridges, Mozart, and champagne.

Types of accounting

Activities in accounting can be divided into several types, as now explained.

Bookkeeping

Whatever the eventual use of accounting information, the raw data first needs to be collected. Each time a shop sells something, a bank lends money or a manufacturer pays the wages, a record must be kept. The process of recording all the transactions is called bookkeeping. It used to be done in a series of pieces of paper (journals) and large books (ledgers), but is now generally done by computer. Either way, the technique used is nearly always 'double-entry bookkeeping', which is an Italian invention of the thirteenth century. It is famous for its debits and credits.

Financial accounting

Financial accounting is the use of accounting data in order to calculate and report the cash flows, profit and financial position of an entity. The word 'entity' is used here in order to include all types of private-sector and public-sector organizations. Financial accounting information is prepared in summarized form for people outside of the entity, such as shareholders. The process of sending such information is called financial reporting. To take the example of shareholders in a company, the financial reporting helps them to assess the success of their company and its managers, and it helps them to make investment decisions. The financial reports include an income statement and a balance sheet.

3

Auditing

In many entities, especially large ones, most of the owners are not the day-to-day managers. This is why financial reporting is necessary. However, there is a horrible risk that the managers (including the accountants in the company) will overstate success or hide problems when they report to outsiders. This is why independent experts are needed to check on the information reported by the managers. Many accountants work in the field of auditing.

Management accounting

The information collected by the bookkeepers can also be used to present detailed information about individual products, factories, or managers. This is used by managers inside the company in order to make decisions about prices, volumes of production, locations for expansion, and who to promote. It is also used to control the company.

Management accounting can be divided into several types of activity, including cost accounting (which concentrates on finding out the cost of particular units or types of production) and budgetary control (which identifies inputs and outputs with particular managers in order to help them to make operational decisions).

Accountancy bodies and accountancy firms

As in many other fields of work, accountants have formed societies to advance their interests. An early example of a body of accountants was the Collegio dei Rasonati in Venice from 1581. The ship-building works at the Arsenale were so vital to the success of Venice that the state founded this body of auditors to control the costs and detect any mismanagement. However, the earliest private-sector accountancy bodies were founded in the UK in the nineteenth century, for reasons to be examined in Chapter 2. Table 1 shows some examples of these bodies around the world.

Table 1. Examples of accountancy bodies, age, and size

Country	Body	Founding date[a]	Approx. number of members (1000s), 2010
Australia	CPA Australia	1952 (1886)	132
	Institute of Chartered Accountants in Australia	1928 (1885)	54
Canada	Canadian Institute of Chartered Accountants	1902 (1880)	78
China	Chinese Insitute of Certified Public Accountants	1988	140
France	Ordre des Experts Comptables	1942	19
Germany	Institut der Wirtschaftsprüfer	1932	13
Japan	Japanese Institute of Certified Public Accountants	1948 (1927)	20
Netherlands	Nederlands Instituut van Registeraccountants	1967 (1895)	14
New Zealand	New Zealand Society of Accountants	1909 (1894)	32

(continued)

Table 1. Continued

Country	Body	Founding date[a]	Approx. number of members (1000s), 2010
Sweden	Föreningen Auktoriserade Revisorer; Svenska Revisorsamfundet	2006 (1899)	6
United Kingdom and Ireland	Institute of Chartered Accountants in England and Wales	1880 (1870)	136
	Institute of Chartered Accountants of Scotland	1951 (1854)	19
	Association of Chartered Certified Accountants	1939 (1891)	140
	Chartered Accountants Ireland	1888	20
United States	American Institute of Certified Public Accountants	1887	348

Note: [a] Dates of earliest predecessor bodies in brackets

International comparisons of statistics, as in many fields, are fraught with difficulty. For example, the German body in Table 1 only has practising auditors as members, whereas the UK's Chartered Institute of Management Accountants has very few auditors (and only if they are also members of another body). Nevertheless, it is clear that accountants are a speciality of the English-speaking world. In extreme cases, such as Australia, New Zealand, and the UK, accountants are very numerous (e.g. nearly 1 per cent of the population in New Zealand). The big accountancy firms (see later) are the largest employers of new university graduates in these places. Accountancy is the most common background for chief executives of companies in these countries, and several accountants are members of parliament. At the other extreme (e.g. Germany), even the head of accounting in BMW or Lufthansa is unlikely to be a trained accountant but will be a business graduate or engineer instead.

Some accountants who offer professional services (in fields such as insolvency, audit, and tax) operate alone, but others have joined together in partnerships. The four famous accountancy firms can all trace their earliest origins to the UK, although they are all now larger in the USA. In alphabetical order, these firms are: Deloitte, Ernst & Young, KPMG, and PwC.

The components of their names are as follows:

- Deloitte is legally 'Deloitte Touche Tohmatsu Limited', a UK company. The 'Deloitte' comes from a Londoner (William Deloitte), the 'Touche' from the Edinburgh born George Touche, and the 'Tohmatsu' from a Japanese auditor.

- A. C. Ernst worked in Cleveland; Arthur Young worked first in Glasgow and then New York. The global executive office of Ernst & Young is in London.

- KPMG once stood for Klynveld (Dutch), Peat (London), Marwick (Glasgow, then New York), and Goerdeler (German). For legal and tax reasons, KPMG is based in Switzerland.

- PwC resulted from various mergers of firms named after 'Price', 'Waterhouse', and the four 'Cooper' brothers (all from London).

Rules

Some areas of accounting work do not need rules to govern them. In particular, management accounting is done inside an organization, and can be arranged exactly to suit its particular circumstances. However, financial reporting is used by many investors and others, so there are advantages in its being regulated. In much of the world, various forms of law impose 'accounting standards' on companies, particularly on listed companies. The standards are written by committees of accountants; the most important being the International Accounting Standards Board (IASB).

Related subject areas

The core work of the accountancy firms is audit, but the UK firms first specialized in insolvency work (the rescuing or winding up of businesses), and still carry this out. It is now euphemistically called 'corporate recovery'; and audit is part of 'assurance'. Throughout the world, the accountancy firms also have many staff working on tax. In some countries (e.g. Germany and Italy), tax and accounting are very closely linked, so that expertise in one field automatically implies expertise in the other. In other countries (e.g. the USA and the UK), the main purpose of accounting is to give useful financial reports to investors. So, accounting is not primarily designed for tax calculations. Although some accounting numbers in these latter countries are used for tax, there are many adjustments to make, which are based on tax law. In the USA, tax is more the province of lawyers than of accountants.

Many employees of the accountancy firms (including many qualified accountants) work in consultancy, although frequently this is connected to accounting numbers. Another field related to accounting is finance, which is concerned with the raising of money and how to best use it. Finance addresses such questions as: If a company wishes to expand, should it borrow money or should it get more money from its owners? If a company has spare money, should it invest in new projects, pay dividends to the shareholders, buy back its own shares, or pay off its debts? How much does a company's share price move when it announces a particular level of profit? What strategy should investors in stocks and bonds use in order to out-perform the general stock market?

This book focusses on the central areas of accounting (financial reporting and management accounting) and does not have space to examine the areas of insolvency, tax, consultancy, and finance.

The reporting entity

At one extreme, a business can be run by a single person with no other owners and no organization which is legally separate from the person. This business might be called a 'sole trader'. The trader has unlimited liability for the debts of the business and pays personal income tax on the profits. If the business is to be sold, then the trader must sell the individual assets and liabilities because there is no separate legal entity to sell. Nevertheless, the trader keeps the accounts for the business distinct from other personal activities. Otherwise, the success of the business and the basis for calculating tax will be unclear.

As the business becomes larger, it may be useful to have some joint owners (partners) who can contribute skills and money. The business then becomes a partnership, which is formalized by a contract between the partners which specifies their rights and duties. In common law countries, such as the United States, Australia and England (though not Scotland), a partnership does not have separate legal existence for most purposes. So, the partners are legally responsible for its assets and liabilities, and they pay tax on their share of the profits. Nevertheless, it is possible to set up a 'limited liability partnership' (LLP) and, for example, many accountancy firms have done so. The purpose of this is to seek to protect the partners from some part of the liabilities of the partnership in the event of a legal case being brought against it. In Roman law countries (such as most countries in continental Europe, in South America and Japan), some forms of partnership do have separate legal status, although generally the partners still pay the business's tax.

The complete legal separation of owners from their business is achieved by setting up a company, usually with limited liability for the owners. The ownership of the company is denoted by shares, which can be transferred from one owner (a shareholder) to another without affecting the company's existence. A company is a separate legal entity from its owners. The company can buy and sell assets, and it pays tax on its own profit.

In many jurisdictions, including the whole of the EU and South Africa, companies can be either private or public. A private company is not allowed to create a public market in its shares, so they have to be exchanged by private agreement between the owners and the company. Many small businesses are set up as private companies. By contrast, public companies are allowed to have their shares traded on markets. Some designations of companies are shown in Table 2. Public companies have to comply with some extra rules because they can offer shares to the public but these rules vary by country and are of no importance for our purposes.

The biggest form of market for shares is a stock exchange. Companies that are listed (quoted) on a stock exchange have extra rules to obey coming from stock exchanges, regulators of stock exchanges or other sources.

There are some linguistic problems here. First, the English word 'company' has no exact equivalent in some other languages. For example, the French *société* and the German *Gesellschaft* are

Table 2. Some EU company names

	Private	Public
Belgium, France, Luxembourg	Société à responsabilité limitée (Sarl)	Société anonyme (SA)
Denmark	Anpartsselskab (ApS)	Aktieselskab (AS)
Finland	Osakeyhtiö-yksityinen (Oy)	Osakeyhtiö julkinen (Oyj)
Germany, Austria	Gesellschaft mit beschränkter Haftung (GmbH)	Aktiengesellschaft (AG)
Greece	Etairía periorismenis efthynis (EPE)	Anonymos etairía (AE)
Italy	Società a responsabilità limitata (SRL)	Società per azioni (SpA)
Netherlands, Belgium	Besloten vennootschap (BV)	Naamloze vennootschap (NV)
Norway	Aksjeselskap (AS)	Almennaksjeselskap (ASA)
Portugal	Sociedade por quotas (Lda)	Sociedade anónima (SA)
Spain	Sociedad de responsabilidad limitada (SRL)	Sociedad anónima (SA)
Sweden	Aktiebolag-privat	Aktiebolag-publikt
United Kingdom, Ireland	Private limited company (Ltd)	Public limited company (plc)

broader terms, also covering partnerships. Another problem is that the term 'public company' tends to be used, particularly in the United States, to mean *listed* company. It is true that only public limited companies in the UK (and their equivalents elsewhere in Europe) are *allowed* to be listed, but most such companies choose not to be. So, most UK public companies are not listed.

In practice, nearly all the world's important companies are really groups of entities which operate together. Let us take the example of Nokia, the Finnish telephone company. The public can buy shares in a company called Nokia Oy. It is a legal entity, and it transacts business in its own right. However, much of the activity goes on in subsidiary legal entities in Finland and many other countries. For example, there are major manufacturing subsidiaries in seven countries. These subsidiaries are legal entities. They pay taxes locally. They pay dividends up to the top parent company.

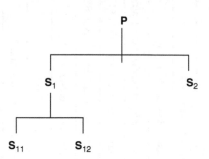

2. A simple group

A simplified example is shown as Figure 2. There are five legal entities: one parent (P), two direct subsidiaries (S_1 and S_2) and two subsidiaries of subsidiary S_1. A subsidiary entity is one controlled by a parent entity. The parent and the subsidiaries therefore act together as a group. Accountants prepare 'consolidated' financial statements for the group as a whole. Approximately speaking, this involves adding together the financial statements of all the group members, e.g. the five companies in Figure 2.

Chapter 2
The international evolution of accounting

International contributions to accounting

Among other things, this chapter addresses the following questions: How have different countries contributed to the development of accounting over the millennia? What are the purposes of accounting? How do the different purposes affect how accounting works? What are the key features of double-entry bookkeeping?

This section outlines some major examples of how different countries have contributed to the development of accounting over the centuries, in approximately chronological order. The key points will be explained and expanded upon later in the chapter.

When archaeologists uncover ancient remains in the Middle East, almost anything with writing or numbers on it is a form of accounting: expenses of wars, feasts or construction projects; or lists of taxes due or paid. It is now well documented that the origins of written numbers and written words are closely associated with the need to keep account. One major reason for needing to keep account is so that the stewards of resources can later give an account to the owner of what they did with the resources. Originally, this was the high officials giving account to temple complexes or kings. Now, it is the directors of a company giving account to its shareholders.

The Romans developed forms of accounting from which, for example, farm profits could be calculated. Later, India and the Arab world had sophisticated numbering systems and accounting records. However, it is probably in northern Italy in the thirteenth century that the ultimate system was invented: double-entry bookkeeping. This was driven by the increasing complexity of business, such as the setting up of partnerships and foreign branches. Later still, France led in the development of legal control over accounting in the seventeenth century.

The existence of a wealthy merchant class and the need for large investment for major projects led to public subscription of share capital in seventeenth-century Amsterdam. This creates the need to report to large numbers of shareholders who are not the managers. Then, the industrial revolution caused the need to get even bigger and to raise massive funds. This meant a growing separation of ownership from management, which led to the requirement for auditors to check on the management in nineteenth-century Britain. Scotland pioneered the accountancy profession.

Germany gave us standardized formats for financial statements at the beginning of the twentieth century. Then, the United States contributed consolidation of financial statements for groups, management accounting, and complex financial reporting such as the capitalization of leases (to be explained later). The United Kingdom invented the 'true and fair view' requirement for financial reporting, which is now the top principle of accounting in many countries. In the late twentieth century, Japan contributed greatly to managerial accounting and control.

The common feature of all these international influences on accounting is that commercial developments have brought accounting advances. Not surprisingly, leading commercial nations in any period are the leading innovators in accounting.

Debits and credits

The nuts and bolts of accounting are debits and credits. As we will see, the debits and credits fit together in an algebraic way (the totals are equal). Since they are recorded numerically, they can be manipulated arithmetically (for example, a profit can be calculated). Debits and credits are the positive and negative elements of the double-entry system but they pre-date it.

Let us go back to northern Italy before double-entry was invented; for example, to Florence in 1250 AD. The city then, as now, specialized in small-scale businesses which produced high value products, such as fashion goods. Suppose that we are looking at a business which is the equivalent of Prada, Gucci, Versace, or Dolce & Gabbana. The business can be described with a few basic facts as seen in Box 1.

Box 1

- The business is owned and managed by a single man (e.g. Signor Marco Pazzi) or his family.

- Raw materials (e.g. wool) come from far away (e.g. England) and are not paid for in cash when they arrive. Signor Pazzi would be mad to send florins on the long journey back to England. He might send a letter of credit to his supplier, King Henry, which can be used in a branch of the Medici bank in London.

- The customers are mostly Florentine nobles, merchants and clerics, plus a few from Pisa, Milan and Venice. They seldom pay cash immediately; it would be rude to ask them.

Under these circumstances, what sort of accounting records are needed? Remember that accounting takes time and valuable paper, so Pazzi will only want to record what is really necessary. We can start by working out what is not necessary, as in Box 2.

However, what is absolutely necessary in order to avoid commercial chaos is a record of how much the customers owe Pazzi and how much Pazzi owes others. Without such records, Pazzi will forget to demand payments from customers and he will not know whether demands on him from suppliers are justified. Pazzi must keep the records in detail (dates, times, amounts, currencies, etc.). Good records will be persuasive when talking to customers and suppliers, or if it is ever necessary to go to court.

So, Pazzi keeps one piece of paper for each customer and each supplier. Naturally, he begins with the sign of the cross. He uses Roman numerals because foreign Arabic/Indian numerals have not arrived in general use yet. An abacus is used for adding and subtracting. It works with multiples of five and ten, which suits Roman numerals (and fingers) perfectly.

Suppose that, so far, King Henry has sent 300 florins of wool on January 5th; and Signor Bardi has bought 21 florins worth of garments on January 10th and another 12 florins worth on February 3rd. No cash has changed hands. The records will then show:

King Henry		Bardi	
He trusts		**He owes**	
v Jan. CCC		x Jan.	XXI
		iii Feb.	XII

Of course, Pazzi writes in medieval Tuscan, so instead of 'he owes', Pazzi writes 'debit'; and for 'he trusts', Pazzi writes 'credit'. So Bardi is a debitor (a debtor; he must pay Pazzi) and King Henry is a creditor (he trusts Pazzi to pay him later).

King Henry	Bardi
credit	*debit*
CCC	XXI
	XII

You might be wondering why the debits (such as Bardi's) are on the left of accounts and the credits are on the right. Some bad aspects of 'left' can be seen in Box 3.

So, whose balance shall we put on the left: that of the wretched customer who has not yet paid us, or that of the kind supplier who has trusted us to pay later? Hence, the debtors' balances are entered on the left.

Pazzi never crosses any numbers out; that would lead to confusion and allegations of fraud. Pazzi never uses minuses, since minuses do not exist yet. When Bardi pays Pazzi (perhaps 50 florins), the amount is recorded on the right of Bardi's account. It is to Bardi's credit that he has paid. When Pazzi pays the King (perhaps 120 florins), the amount is recorded on the left of the King's account. At any moment, Pazzi can balance each account to work out how much is due to or from any party. In summary, including the cash transfers just mentioned, the result is:

3. 'The Last Supper' by Andrea del Castagno

King Henry			Bardi	
debit	credit		debit	credit
CXX	CCC		XXI	L
			XII	

From single to double

You will have noticed that the earlier accounting system records each transaction once. Furthermore, the debits do not equal the credits. There is no reason why they should. However, during the thirteenth century, business became more complex as seen in Box 4.

Box 4

- Co-owners (partners) and employees, who were not members of the immediate family, were brought in. This increased the chance of dishonesty, which meant that fuller records were useful.

- The arrival of the partners meant that it became necessary to calculate profit, so that it could be shared.

- Some branches of the business were set up far away (in Venice, Rome, Paris, Bruges, and even London). This increased the need for records. There were multiple currencies, and sometimes goods or credit notes were in transit between branches for weeks.

- The cash and the inventory were now large. Particular employees looked after them. It became important to have a record of how much cash and inventory there *should be* so that this could be compared to how much there actually was. The cashier and the stock man could be regarded as debtors of the business. For example, when cash is received by the business, the cashier takes it and then 'owes' it to the business.

Some transactions can now easily be seen as a double entry. For example, if a customer pays some money into the business to settle his account, we record: debit cashier; credit customer. Or, if the bank lends the business some money, we record: debit cashier; credit bank.

It will be useful to do some introductory double entry now. Suppose that a company's very first transaction is: the owners put 40 cash into the company. So, two things have happened:

1. The business has 40 more cash.
2. The owners have an interest of 40 in the company.

The top part of Figure 4 shows the balance sheet after this transaction.

Balance Sheet (I)	
Cash + 40	Owner + 40

Balance Sheet (II)	
Cash 40	Owner 40
+ 60	Debt + 60

4. **Starting a business**

Now, suppose that the company needs more money to start operating, so it borrows 60 from the bank. The company now has cash of 100 and a liability of 60. Balance sheet (II) shows the result, as in the bottom part of Figure 4.

At some point in the thirteenth century, it became clear that *all* transactions could be seen as having two aspects. However, this involved inventing accounts for increasingly abstract things, such as sales or wages. Overall, the accounts could now be divided into three types:

(i) Personal accounts, relating to debtors and creditors.

(ii) Real accounts, relating to such things as land and buildings; buying a building for cash can then be recorded as: *debit* building, *credit* cash.

(iii) Nominal accounts, relating to sales or wages; paying the wages in cash is recorded as: *debit* wages, *credit* cash.

An ordered, clerical mind will be attracted to the marvellous result that the total of all the debits equals the total of all the credits. The balance sheet shows the balances on the personal and real accounts: the cash, land, debtors and inventory (the assets), and the claims on those assets held by the owners and the creditors. By looking at all the nominal accounts, the excess of credits over debits is a profit. The profit belongs to the owners. When the profit is added to the owner's interest, the balance sheet will balance. This is a very satisfying result, rather like finishing a Sudoku or a crossword. A more detailed numerical example is given in Chapter 3.

The spread of double entry

Double entry imposes a discipline by requiring a high quality of recording. It enables the calculation of profit and the presentation of the financial position of a business. It provides a satisfying, balancing result. It also alerts the business person to errors in recording, because a lack of balance in the system must mean that an error has been made.

These advantages led to the spread of double entry—first among Italian merchants. The oldest surviving records relate to such merchants operating in Provence (1299) and London (1305–8). Double entry spread to non-commercial activities: the administrators of the city of Genoa were using it by the 1340s. There were different versions of double entry, notably a Tuscan one and a Venetian one. The latter had the clearer two-sided presentation, which is seen in the boxes above.

However, the method spread somewhat slowly round the world. For example, the administrators of the city of Bristol did not adopt a full double entry system until 1785. Bristol is a good English analogy for Genoa; they were both important trading ports. Boats were going between the cities throughout the four and a half centuries that it took for double entry to pass from Genoa town hall to Bristol town hall. Obviously, Bristol knew about double entry, but just thought it was not necessary. Incidentally, the British parliament eventually abandoned tally sticks in favour of double entry. When the old tally sticks were burnt, the fire got out of control and destroyed the Houses of Parliament in 1834, as recorded by Turner in a painting.

Even for commercial activities, double entry arrived slowly in Europe, and then spread to America, Japan, and so on, over the centuries. One aid to its transfer was textbooks. The earliest surviving textbook is a section of a massive work on everything mathematical by Luca Pacioli, a Franciscan friar and mathematics professor. The book, *Summa de Arithmetica, Geometria, Proportioni et Proportionalità*, was published in Venice in 1494. The book was in Italian not Latin, so it was more easily understood by merchants. And it was printed. The double entry section formed the basis of later works in Flemish, French, and English.

5. 'Luca Pacioli' by Jacopo de' Barbari

A portrait of Pacioli is shown as Figure 5. It has been much
copied. For example, it forms the cover of Australia's oldest
academic accounting journal, *Abacus*; and it has been used in
several professional accounting publications. Pacioli has been
called 'the father of double entry', but this is somewhat misleading
given that double entry was conceived 200 years before his
seminal work.

Publication and accountability

After the Industrial Revolution and the victories of Nelson and
Wellington, Britain became the 'top nation', commercially and
militarily. Legislation to ease the creation of limited liability
companies in 1844 led to widespread ownership of many large
companies. In order to protect the shareholders and creditors

from potential malpractice by the directors of companies, publication of accounting information was required.

Even so, some company failures involved massive losses, for example the City of Glasgow Bank in 1878. This led to the requirement for audit by outside experts, initially for banks, and then for all companies from 1900. Britain had invented the widespread publication of audited financial statements. Throughout the twentieth century, Companies Acts gradually introduced more accounting regulations. These eventually included EU attempts at harmonization.

America takes over

While Britannia had been ruling the waves, American companies had been waiving the rules. Indeed, when the Wall Street Crash overtook US commerce in 1929, there were hardly any requirements on publication or audit, even for the largest listed companies. One of the reactions to the catastrophe was the creation, in 1934, of the world's toughest and oldest stock market regulator, the Securities and Exchange Commission (SEC). The US audit profession then began to write its own reporting and auditing rules, eventually called 'standards', apparently following the term used in the British process which started much later, in 1969.

In 1973, the US profession handed standard-setting on financial reporting to a new independent body, the Financial Accounting Standards Board (FASB). At present, the SEC accepts the FASB's standards as part of its required rules, called 'generally accepted accounting principles' (US GAAP).

New York still has by far the world's largest stock exchange, in terms of the number of listed companies and their market capitalization. There are thousands of companies and millions of investors in shares and in debt securities (i.e. bonds, whereby the company promises to re-pay amounts to the holders). Gradually, by the 1970s, a newly clear purpose for financial reporting was identified: to give useful information to investors to help them to make economic decisions by predicting a company's cash flows.

So, during the twentieth century, the USA contributed stock market regulators, private-sector standard-setters, and a user decision-making focus for financial reporting. The FASB was also generally ahead of the rest of the world in writing rules for any particular type of transaction.

Accounting practice becomes international

As already explained, many nations have contributed to developments in accounting. However, this does not mean that financial reporting was necessarily done in the same way across the world. Until the 1970s, there seemed to be no need for this. However, as usual, commercial developments led to accounting developments.

From the 1970s onwards, 'globalization' gathered pace. For decades, British groups had owned American subsidiaries, but now British banks started lending to American companies, and British pension funds started buying American shares. Of course, the traffic was both ways, and it now involved Japan, Germany, France, and many other countries.

A major purpose of financial reporting is to enable investors (such as shareholders or bankers) to compare companies. However, this is frustrated if financial reporting practices differ on an international basis. Chapter 4 will give examples of the differences. By the 1970s, governments and accountants had become interested in international 'harmonization' of financial reporting. In the Common Market (now the European Union), proposals were drawn up to change laws to achieve harmonization. This alarmed accountants in the UK, who did not want to lose control of accounting, especially to French or German governments. So, in 1973, the year in which the UK joined the Common Market, the British accountancy bodies (see Table 2 in Chapter 1) led the development of an International Accounting Standards Committee (IASC); the accountancy bodies of nine nations founded the IASC.

For 20 years, the IASC produced international standards which few companies obeyed. Then, from 1994, some large German companies began to use international standards. Political developments were behind this, just as they lay behind the foundation of the IASC. When Germany re-unified in 1990, this led to international expansion of many large German companies, and to capital-raising in New York and London. Most large German companies had adopted international standards by 2000. This was a prelude to the EU adopting international standards for listed companies for 2005 onwards. The EU wanted common standards in order to integrate and boost European stock markets. The EU had tried the route of changing laws but this was slow and ineffective because of political compromises over the content of the rules.

In 2001, the IASC was replaced by an independent private-sector trust, the International Accounting Standards Board (IASB), which was modelled on the FASB. Its standards (International Financial Reporting Standards (IFRS)) are now required for the financial reporting of listed companies in about 90 countries, including the EU, Australia, Brazil, and Canada. In some other countries (e.g. Japan and Switzerland), IFRS is allowed. In yet other countries (e.g. China), national rules are now close to IFRS. However, IFRS is not accepted for US companies. The US regulator (the SEC) believes that the greater detail of US GAAP is more appropriate in the USA, where legal cases involving accounting are much more common than they are anywhere else. It seems likely that IFRS and US GAAP will remain distinct sets of requirements: a very large proportion of listed companies follows either one or the other.

Chapter 3
The fundamentals of financial accounting

The first two chapters of this book looked at the role of accounting, the types of accounting, and the development of accounting over thousands of years. This chapter explores the basic ideas of financial accounting: the way accounting actually works, the logic behind the double-entry recording system, and the contents of the basic financial statements (balance sheet, income statement, and cash flow statement). The objective of this chapter is to enable readers to understand accounting well enough in order to make use of it. Among other things, the chapter addresses the following questions: What does a balance sheet try to show? Why does it balance? How is it that any one transaction has two accounting effects? Which costs lead to assets and which lead to expenses? How can a profitable company go bust because of a lack of cash?

The balance sheet

A balance sheet is a document designed to show the state of affairs of an entity at a particular date. Its official International Financial Reporting Standards (IFRS) name is 'statement of financial position'. The balance sheet is the culmination of a long and complex process of recording and then analysing all the transactions of an entity. If the balance sheet does not balance, mistakes have been made during the preparation process; and they will have to be found.

The public tends to regard the balance sheet, which contains lots of big numbers and yet apparently magically arrives at the same figure twice, as proof of both the complicated nature of accountancy and of the technical competence and reliability of the accountants and auditors involved. However, reduced to its simplest, a balance sheet consists of two lists. The first is a list of the *resources* that are under the control of the entity—a list of *assets*. The word 'asset' derives from the Latin *ad satis* via Norman French *assetz* (sufficient), in the sense that such items could be used to satisfy debts. One modern definition of 'asset' is that used by the International Accounting Standards Board (IASB):

> An asset is a resource controlled by the entity as a result of past events and from which future economic benefits are expected to flow to the entity.

Note that the definition refers to 'control' not to 'ownership'. This was a conscious decision by accountants in the English-speaking world. For example, American Airlines or British Airways do not own many of their planes. For tax or other reasons, they lease the planes from financial institutions. However, the airlines control the use of the planes for most of their economic lives. Accountants treat the planes as assets of the airlines not of the finance companies which own them.

The reference to a past event is included, in the above definition of an asset, so that accountants can identify the asset. It also helps them to attribute a monetary value to it. The final part of the definition (expected benefits) is the point of the asset: no benefits, no asset.

The second list of items on the balance sheet shows where the assets came from, in other words, the monetary amounts of the

Table 3. The contents of a balance sheet

First list: resources controlled	Second list: sources
Assets	Claims

sources from which the entity obtained its present stock of *resources*. Since those sources will require repayment or recompense in some way, it follows that this second list can also be regarded as a list of *claims* by others against the resources of the entity. These terms can be summarized as in Table 3. Since both lists relate to the same business at the same point in time, the totals of each list are equal and the balance sheet must balance. It is defined and constructed so that it has to balance. It represents two ways of looking at the same situation.

Beginning at the beginning

When a new business entity is created, the starting position is that there is no balance sheet because there is no entity. The new business will have to be owned by someone. This outside person or other body will put some cash (a resource) into the entity as ownership capital, often called *equity capital*. This is the source of the cash which the entity now owns. Suppose that capital of €100,000 is put in to begin the operation. This leads to the balance sheet shown in Table 4. Notice that the cash is an asset, in other words, a resource, whereas the equity capital is a claim on the business by the owner, although usually there is no legal obligation for a business to repay its owners unless the business is closed down.

Table 4. Balance sheet of a new entity

Resources (€)		Claims (€)	
Cash	100,000	Equity	100,000

Suppose the entity runs a retail shop which after

1. the first input of capital of €100,000

undertakes the following transactions:

2. borrows €60,000 from the bank
3. buys property for €50,000
4. buys inventory (goods to be sold again) costing €45,000, paying cash
5. sells one-third of the quantity of this inventory for €35,000, on credit (i.e. with the customer promising to pay later)
6. pays wages for the period, in cash, of €4,000
7. receives €16,000 of the money due from the customer
8. buys inventory costing €25,000, on credit (i.e. the entity will pay later).

In return for the extra resource of €60,000 of cash, Transaction 2 creates an additional claim of €60,000 in the form of a loan from the bank. Amounts that must be paid to outsiders (not to the owners) are called 'liabilities'. This word derives from the word 'liable', meaning tied, bound, or obliged by law. The IASB defines a liability as:

> a present obligation of the entity arising from past events, the settlement of which is expected to result in an outflow from the entity of resources embodying economic benefits.

This portrays a liability as a negative version of an asset. Claims by the owners, which are not expected to be paid back to them, are not called liabilities but owner's *equity* (or various similar expressions).

All the eight transactions can be analysed in this way, as shown in Table 5. For example, Transactions 1 to 4 each involve changes in resources and claims (of matching size).

It would be possible to prepare a new balance sheet after each transaction. After Transaction 2, the balance sheet would look as in Table 6. The order of items in a balance sheet in many countries (e.g. those in the European Union) is traditionally that longer term items are shown first. By contrast, in North America, Australia, and Japan, balance sheets begin with cash.

Transaction 3 involves using some of the cash to buy a long-term asset, a property from which to operate the business. One resource (part of the cash) is turned into another resource (property), so that the total resources and claims remain the same as they were, and still equal (see Table 7).

We can now turn to Transaction 4 in the earlier list, and ask: which new resources or claims result from this transaction? Like Transaction 3, Transaction 4 does not involve any new or additional resources, only a *change* in them: €45,000 which had previously been part of the store of cash has now been changed to a different resource/asset—inventory. Therefore, total resources and total claims remain constant at €160,000 (see Table 8).

Transaction 5 is rather more complicated. There are some easy aspects. First, one third of the inventory has been sold, and so the inventory figure must be reduced from €45,000 to €30,000. Second, the customer has agreed to pay the entity €35,000. This does not mean that the entity has the cash; it does, however, have the *right* to receive the cash. This is an additional resource of the

Table 5. An analysis of the transactions (in €000)

Transaction	Resources (€)			Claims (€)	
	Cash	Receivables	Other assets	Outsiders: liabilities	Owner: capital and profit
1. Original capital	+100				+100
2. Borrowing	+60			+60	
3. Buy property	-50		+50		
4. Buy inventory for cash	-45		+45		
5. Sell some inventory		+35	-15		+20 (i.e. 35 – 15)
6. Pay wages	-4				-4
7. Customer pays	+18	-18			
8. Buy inventory on credit			+25	+25	
TOTALS	+79	+17	+105	+85	+116

Table 6. Balance sheet after loan

Resources (€)		Claims (€)	
Cash	160,000	Equity	100,000
		Loan	60,000
Total	160,000	Total	160,000

Table 7. The balance sheet after buying property

Resources (€)		Claims (€)	
Property	50,000	Equity	100,000
Cash	110,000	Loan	60,000
Total	160,000	Total	160,000

Table 8. The balance sheet after buying inventory

Resources (€)		Claims (€)	
Property	50,000	Equity	100,000
Inventory	45,000	Loan	60,000
Cash	65,000		
Total	160,000	Total	160,000

business, an additional asset. The business has something extra, namely the valuable and useful right to receive this cash. The €35,000 represents the receivable (or debtor; that is, the customer who has an obligation to pay and from whom the business has a right to receive the additional asset). The conclusion as regards Transaction 5 is that one resource has fallen by €15,000, and a new resource has appeared in the amount of €35,000. This means that total resources have risen by €20,000. However, we cannot have a resource without a claim. What is the origin of this increase in resources of €20,000?

In intuitive terms, it should be clear what has happened. The business has sold something for more than it had originally paid for it. Through its operations, the business has turned an asset recorded as €15,000 (i.e. the cost of one-third of the physical amount of inventory) into an asset of €35,000 (i.e. the receivable). The business has made a profit. Numerically, in order to make the balance sheet balance, it is necessary to put this profit of €20,000 on to the opposite side of the balance sheet, as a claim (see Table 9). Would this make sense in logical as well as numerical terms?

The answer is 'yes', as can be seen by looking back at the 'second list' in Table 3. Extra 'assets' have come from the profitable trading of the enterprise. The profits made by the business are for the ultimate benefit of the owner, and therefore can be said to belong to the owner of the business. They can be regarded as an extra claim against the business by the owner. At its simplest, the profit can be measured numerically as an increase in the assets. The profit change shown in the transition from Tables 8 to 9 is not accompanied by a change in the amount of cash, because cash has not yet been received from the customer.

Table 9. The balance sheet after selling some inventory

Resources (€)		Claims (€)	
Property	50,000	Equity	100,000
Inventory	30,000	Profit	20,000
Receivable	35,000	Loan	60,000
Cash	65,000		
Total	180,000	Total	180,000

It should be obvious by now that each transaction has at least two effects on the financial position. This should also be clear from the analysis in Table 5. Note how Transaction 5 (selling some inventory) has been recorded there.

Why it matters

Without good records of the receivables (debtors) and loans and other payables (creditors), the business might forget to demand its money from debtors, and would not know whether a creditor's claim for money should be paid. Financial disaster would follow.

Moving on to Transaction 6 (paying wages), two numerical alterations are needed to the balance sheet in order to incorporate the new event. First, the amount of cash that the entity controls as asset goes down by €4,000. This sum of money has physically been paid out by the entity, so the amount remaining must be €4,000 less than it was before. Has this €4,000 been turned into some other resource/asset? The answer seems to be 'no'. The wages relate to the past, and therefore they represent the reward given by the entity for work, for labour hours that *have already been used up*.

The wages represent services provided and already totally consumed by the business as part of the process of generating profit in the trading period, which we had previously recorded at €20,000. This needs to be taken into account in calculating the overall profit or gain made by the entity through the operations over this trading period. Thus €4,000 needs to be deducted from the profit figure of €20,000 in order to show a fair measure of the profit from the operations of the entity made for the benefit of the owner (see Table 10). The wages involved a reduction in assets (cash fell) and the recognition of a reduced claim by the owners (profits fell). This reduction in the measure of profit can also be called an *expense*.

Table 10. The balance sheet after paying wages

Resources (€)		Claims (€)	
Property	50,000	Equity	100,000
Inventory	30,000	Profit	16,000
Receivable	35,000	Loan	60,000
Cash	61,000		
Total	176,000	Total	176,000

Transaction 7 (customer pays €18,000) is straightforward. The starting position is that there was a receivable—an asset, an amount owed to the business—of €35,000. Some of this money is now received by the business. This tells us two things: first, the cash figure has increased by €18,000; second, the business is no longer owed the €18,000 because it has already received it. The receivable therefore needs to be reduced by €18,000 (see Table 11). In summary, we have an increase in the asset 'cash' and a decrease in the asset 'receivable', both by the same amount. Total assets/resources remain the same, and therefore total claims/sources remain the same too.

Table 11. The balance sheet after receipt from customer

Resources (€)		Claims (€)	
Property	50,000	Equity	100,000
Inventory	30,000	Profit	16,000
Receivable	17,000	Loan	60,000
Cash	79,000		
Total	176,000	Total	176,000

Table 12. The balance sheet after further purchase

Resources (€)		Claims (€)	
Property	50,000	Equity	100,000
Inventory	55,000	Profit	16,000
Receivable	19,000	Loan	60,000
Cash	77,000	Payable	25,000
Total	201,000	Total	201,000

Looking back to the earlier list of transactions, we can find the details of Transaction 8. In this final transaction, the business buys more inventory for €25,000, and so the inventory figure in the balance sheet—the resource/asset of inventory—rises by €25,000. This has not yet been paid for and so there is no corresponding reduction in any of the other resources. The total of resources therefore rises by €25,000—and so, of course, does the total claims because the business owes the supplier for the extra inventory. The extra claim is known as a payable (or a creditor). This is shown in Table 12.

In Table 12, the equity is €116,000 (the sum of the first two items: the original capital plus the profit), whereas the liabilities to the third parties are €85,000 (the sum of the last two items). The right-hand side of the balance sheet of Table 12 could be redrawn to show the two types of claims, as shown in Table 13. Notice how this fits with the totals of the claims in Table 5.

The income statement

It has been shown that any transaction, event or adjustment can be recorded to produce a new and updated balance sheet. It would be possible to carry on this process in the same way for ever, producing an endless series of balance sheets after each transaction. This would not be very practical. Instead, users of

Table 13. The claims side of the balance sheet showing the two types

Equity		
Original	100,000	
Profit	16,000	
		116,000
Liabilities		
Loan	60,000	
Payable	25,000	
		85,000
Total		201,000

accounting information may wish to see balance sheets monthly, half-yearly, or yearly. They may also require information which concentrates on the results of the operating activities of the business. In order to provide this, it is necessary to collect together and summarize those items that are part of the calculation of the performance (or successful operations) of the particular period.

The transaction that led to profit in the above example (the sale of inventory) was expressed as an increase in assets. The transaction that led to a reduction in the profit (the wages) was expressed as a fall in assets. The calculation of profit comprises these positive and negative elements. When the business makes a sale, the proceeds are a positive part of the profit calculation, which is referred to as *revenue*, although the more general word for this and other positive elements is *income*. On the other hand, the operating process involves the consumption of some business resources, an *expense*, which is the negative part. In the example explored in detail earlier, there were two such items of expense. First, the resource of inventory was used, and so the original cost of the used inventory was included as a negative component of the profit calculation. Second, some of the resource of cash was used to pay the wages that had been incurred in the process of the business operations. The two negative components (minus 15 and minus 4) can be seen in the 'owner' column of Table 5.

The income statement (sometimes called the profit and loss account) reports on flows of income and expenses of a period, whereas a balance sheet reports on the financial position (i.e. the stock of resources and claims) at the balance sheet date. Figure 6 shows this diagrammatically. From time to time (at least yearly), the balance sheet is drawn up to show the financial position at that particular moment. For example, in Figure 6, the balance sheet is drawn up at 31 December 20X1 and again at 31 December 20X2. During the year 20X2, assuming that the owners have not introduced or withdrawn capital, the explanation for the changing balance sheet is the operations of the company. Overall, the assets of the company will have grown in 20X2 if there is an excess of income over expenses. The balance of the assets over the liabilities

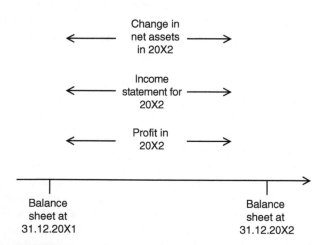

6. **The balance sheet reports on stocks of things; the income statement reports on flows**

is called the net assets. The profit can also be seen as the size of (and the cause of) the increase in net assets in year 20X2.

The logic of the income statement in relation to the balance sheet can be explored by reworking the transactions we used earlier, and by segregating out the expenses and the income from the other aspects of the transactions. Table 14 shows the previous Table 12 but with the profit removed from the right-hand side, and shown in more detail below.

That is, the bottom half of Table 14 shows the detail that led to the profit of €16,000. It shows the income (two sales) and the expenses (the wages and the using up of inventory). It contains all the positive parts of the profit calculation (the income) and all the negative parts of the profit calculation (the expenses). One can

Table 14. Showing the profit in more detail

Resources			Claims	
Assets			**Equity and liabilities**	
Property		50,000	Equity	100,000
Inventory		55,000	Loan	60,000
Receivable		19,000	Payable	25,000
Cash		77,000		
		201,000		185,000
Expenses			**Income**	
Cost of goods sold	15,000		Sales	35,000
Wages	4,000			
		19,000		
		220,000		220,000

extract the bottom half from Table 14 and present this as an income statement—a detailed statement of the result of operating for the period. In total, the income is €35,000 and the expenses are €19,000. The profit is the difference between the two, i.e. €16,000.

The income statement (the whole of the bottom half of Table 14) can be replaced by the single profit number of €16,000 (i.e. €35,000 minus €19,000) on the claims side in the top half of the table which is, of course, the balance sheet. Replacing the income and expenses parts of Table 14 by the single profit figure in the balance sheet leads to Table 12. This profit, as shown earlier, represents an additional ownership claim on the business.

The balance sheet equation

At the start of any period (e.g. at point zero), the assets must equal the claims on them (i.e. equity and liabilities):

$$\text{Assets}_0 = \text{Equity}_0 + \text{Liabilities}_0$$

Then, during period 1, equity rises because the business makes a profit as its income is larger than its expenses. So, equity increases:

$$\text{Equity}_1 - \text{Equity}_0 = \text{Income}_{0 \to 1} - \text{Expenses}_{0 \to 1}$$

The profit will also have led to an increase in net assets, for example inventory was sold for more cash than it had originally cost. We are assuming that no money was put in or taken out by the shareholders in the period. At the end of period 1:

$$\text{Assets}_1 = \text{Equity}_1 + \text{Liabilities}_1$$

Table 14 can be expressed as:

$$\text{Assets}_1 + \text{Expenses}_{0 \to 1} = \text{Equity}_0 + \text{Income}_{0 \to 1} + \text{Liabilities}_1$$

This is another way of saying that the total of the debits equals the total of the credits.

If the balance sheet is re-arranged, it becomes:

$$\text{Assets} - \text{Liabilities} = \text{Equity} = \text{Net assets}$$

That is, the claims of the owner at a point in time (e.g. point 1) are equal to the net assets of the entity. In this model, there are only two factors that can affect capital and cause it to change over time. These are, first, the entity makes a profit (or it could, of course, make a loss) and, second, the owner takes some profit out of the business (by way of cash drawings) or invests extra capital.

In practice

- The self-balancing nature of the accounting system shows up certain types of errors very efficiently.
- The equations are needed in computer systems that run the accounting of businesses.

There is one further implication of all this, concerning the exact definitions of the five elements of the financial statements. The term 'equity' needs no separate definition because it is equal to the difference between assets and liabilities. However, there is a practical problem with the definitions of the other four elements, as will now be explained. In principle, there should be no difficulty, because:

(a) Assets = the resources which have remaining future benefits at the period end and

(b) Expenses = the resources used up in the period.

In other words, some costs create assets and some are expenses, as in Figure 7.

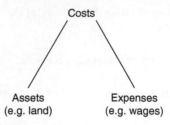

Costs

Assets   Expenses
(e.g. land)   (e.g. wages)

7. Two types of cost

It is time-consuming to have to measure both the assets and the expenses. Judgement is required because there will be doubt about which category to put some costs into. For example, if money is spent on research or advertising, does that create an asset or is it an expense? Consequently, in practice, two solutions are available, as in Box 5.

> **Box 5**
>
> 1. Expenses = resources used up in the period. Therefore, Assets = the rest of the resources.
> 2. Assets = resources with remaining future benefits at the period end. Therefore,
>   Expenses = the rest of the resources.

Solution 1 above, giving primacy to the definition of 'expense' (and 'income'), was the traditional way of doing accounting. It concentrates on transactions in a period. It leaves assets (and changes in their values) as a secondary consideration. However, from the 1970s onwards there have been moves towards Solution 2, giving primacy to the definition of 'asset' (and 'liability'). In principle, this is now the IASB's approach when setting accounting standards. However, accounting is now a mixture of the two. This major point affects many issues and will be taken further in Chapter 4.

How cash flows fit in

In order to understand the operations of an enterprise and to predict its future, it is useful to examine its flows of cash as well as its flows of profit. These two sets of flows are different. For example, in terms of the eight transactions of Table 5, the first four (receiving a capital input, borrowing money, and buying property and inventory) led to inflows and outflows of cash but no profits. The fifth transaction (selling the inventory for later payment by the customer) led to profit but no immediate cash flow.

A statement of cash flows is drawn up for the accounting period. It shows how cash has come in and out in the period, as an explanation of the change in total cash from the beginning to the end of the period. A restatement of the earlier Figure 6 to include cash flows is shown as Figure 8.

In terms of the earlier example, the 'resources' column of Table 5 shows all the transactions involving cash flows. They could be

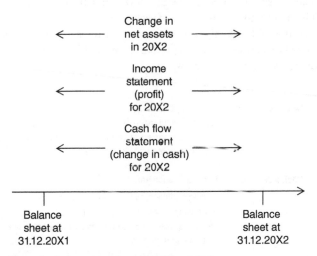

8. **Flows during an example accounting period**

Table 15. A summary of the cash flows in Table 5

	€000
Operating flows (inventory −45, wages −4, customers +16)	−33
Investing flows (property −50)	−50
Financing flows (owner +100, bank +60)	+160
Cash change (starting from no cash)	+77

summarized into three types, as in Table 15: operating, investing, and financing.

It is important to note that a cash increase and profit are not the same things. As noted immediately above, some transactions involve a change in cash with no profit, and some involve a profit with no change in cash. Overall, you will remember from Tables 12 or 13 that the business made a profit of €16,000, but you see from Table 15 that cash increased by €77,000 during the same period. This was caused by raising lots of cash from the owners and the bank. It would certainly be possible for a business to increase cash but make a loss, or to make a profit but have reduced cash (e.g. by buying a lot of non-current assets).

- Cash *decreases* might be 'good', such as:
  - buying useful machines that will last for 10 years
  - paying off loans that required high interest payments
  - doing research and development

- Cash *increases* might be 'bad', such as:
  - selling buildings that are needed for operations
  - borrowing money at a high interest rate
  - giving big discounts to customers if they pay quickly
  - not paying suppliers

9. Cash and success

Accounting

Figure 9 summarizes some of the reasons why decreases in cash might be 'good' and increases in cash might be 'bad'. So, any particular use of cash, and even a net reduction in cash, does not necessarily mean a lack of success. Similarly, increases in cash do not necessarily mean success.

If a company wanted to try to fool outsiders, it might sell all its assets in December and buy them back in January. For a brief period (including 31 December), it would be able to show a large cash balance. This can be called 'window dressing'.

In order to measure success, performance, or profit for a period, a different way from just measuring cash is necessary, which is comparing the income and expenses that relate to the period, as discussed earlier. Nevertheless, although the business is designed to make profit in the long-run, this will not be possible unless it survives in the short-run by making sure that it does not run out of cash. Cash budgeting is examined in Chapter 8.

Chapter 4
Financial reports of listed companies

Among other things, this chapter addresses the following questions: What exactly is an asset? Why are staff not assets? How (and why) are assets divided into groups on balance sheets? Why are different assets measured differently? What is the difference between depreciation and impairment? Why are various expected expenses and losses not accounted for as liabilities? Why are income statements shown in two parts with 'earnings' in the middle? How can an investor decide which company to lend to or buy shares in? How could managers use accounting to mislead investors?

Components of an annual report

A large majority of listed companies in the world follow International Financial Reporting Standards (IFRS) or US 'generally accepted accounting principles' (US GAAP) when preparing their consolidated statements. We will look at these two systems further in Chapter 5. However, for the purposes of this chapter, the two sets of rules are largely the same, except in a few cases as noted.

The annual reports provided by listed companies usually contain hundreds of pages of information, including charts and photographs. We will concentrate here on the 'audited financial statements'. These statements are followed by many notes which provide more detail.

Companies generally provide four types of financial statement:

- balance sheet
- income statement, in two parts
- statement of changes in equity
- cash flow statement.

We have met most of these statements earlier. The statement of changes in equity explains all the changes in the balance sheet over the year: the profits, any new capital provided by the shareholders, and any payments of dividends. In this chapter, we first look in more detail at the key components of the balance sheet: assets and liabilities. This includes examining how they are measured for accounting purposes. Then, we study the income statement, noting that it is split into two parts. Next, we will look at methods of interpreting the financial statements and of comparing one company with another. However, there is then a warning that accounts may mislead. Finally, there is a note on other information included in annual reports.

Assets

In Chapter 3, we began to look at the definition of an asset. In summary, IFRS defines an asset as:

- a resource controlled
- as a result of a past transaction or event
- when future benefit is expected.

You might like to think of examples of the following three different types of resources: (i) used by Company Z but not controlled by it; (ii) controlled by Company Z but not owned by it; and (iii) owned by Company Z but not controlled by it.

An example of (i) is a motorway. This might be very useful to Company Z by reducing its travel costs. The company not only uses the motorway but has a right to do so, but that still does not make the motorway an asset of Z, because Z cannot restrict use by other people.

An example of (ii) is machines or buildings used by Z, which has purchased the right to use them for many years under a lease. Z controls the resource for most of its life. This is treated as Z's asset. An example of (iii) would be the reverse of (ii). That is, suppose that Z owns an asset but has leased it to another company for most of its life. Z has then lost control of the resource, which is therefore not treated as Z's asset.

In some cases, accountants are so uncertain about the value of an asset or whether it will bring any future benefit that the asset is not included in the balance sheet. An example of this is the results of a research project. However, when a project moves on to become applied development and its results can be predicted, it should be put in an IFRS balance sheet. Accountants say that it should be 'recognized' or 'capitalized'.

Types of asset

In terms of physical substance, or lack of it, assets come in three types as seen in Box 6.

Box 6

- Tangible assets, such as property, plant and equipment. These include land, buildings, machines, vehicles, and inventories.
- Intangible assets, such as patents, licences, and software programs.
- Financial assets, such as cash, receivables, shares in other companies, or government bonds.

Accountants also divide all these assets into two categories: (i) non-current, e.g. the company's head office and its machines, and (ii) current, e.g. cash and inventories. The purpose of this is to help readers of the balance sheet to assess future cash flows. The definition of 'current' includes that the asset is cash or expected to turn into cash within one year.

Measuring assets

If an item meets the definition of asset and should be put on the balance sheet, it is then necessary to decide how to measure it. There are various possibilities, outlined in Table 16. The first two (NRV and FV) are versions of today's market value; the NRV is net of selling costs. The next (HC) is what the company actually paid when it bought the asset in the past. The last (DCF) is how much the company expects to benefit (in terms of cash flowing in from selling products, for example) by using the asset in the future. The discounting reduces the size of future flows in order to take account of the time value of money.

You might like to examine the balance sheet of a real company. This is easy to do. You can search the internet for 'investor relations' for any large company, then go to 'annual reports'. The financial statements are usually a little after half-way through an annual report. You will find that the balance sheet starts with assets, divided into non-current and current. Within those two groups, the assets are split into types based loosely on tangible/ intangible/financial. For each type of asset, you might like to guess how the company has valued it (in terms of Table 16).

Table 16. Possible ways of measuring assets

- Selling price now (net realizable value (NRV))

- Market price now (fair value (FV))

- Original cost (historical cost (HC))

- Worth to the business (discounted cash flows (DCF))

Many non-accountants make the reasonable assumption that assets are valued at what they are worth. However, what does that mean? Which of the measures in Table 16 is 'worth'? In practice, any measure except historical cost is difficult to calculate, and different accountants would come to different estimates. Furthermore, it is not clear that today's value (e.g. of selling) is relevant for an asset that will probably not be sold (e.g. the head office). So, in practice, accountants measure most assets on a cost basis. That approach is easy, cheap, and reliable. Of course, the number might not be very relevant for most economic decisions. For a few assets, fair value is used because it can be measured easily: (i) shares, and (ii) in IFRS but not US GAAP, investment property (e.g. an office block that is rented out).

As cost is used to measure most assets, some more details on the meaning of 'cost' are needed. To take the example of inventory, cost includes: the market price of buying the inventory, plus any associated costs or taxes, plus transport costs, plus storage costs, plus labour and materials used to help to turn the inventory into a finished product.

In many cases, the exact cost of a type of inventory is difficult to calculate because, for example, there are many pieces of the inventory that are moving around all the time. In such cases, accountants use a simple assumption, such as that the earliest inventory received is the first one to be used up in production or sales (called 'first in, first out' (FIFO)) or the accountants work out the average cost of all the pieces.

Depreciation of assets

We concluded above that accountants show most non-current assets on a cost basis, for various reasons: cost is more reliable, cost is easier/cheaper to measure, and the company does not intend to sell the asset. However, most assets have limited useful lives: they wear out because of usage (e.g. machines) or because time passes (e.g. patents). The obvious exception is land, which can last forever. For the assets that do wear out, it would not be fair to continue to show them in the balance sheet at the original cost. Also, it would not be fair to charge the whole of the cost of an asset in the measurement of performance on the date of purchase. However, it would also not be fair to make no charge at all, if the asset is gradually being used up in order to make profit.

Therefore, accountants allocate the cost of assets into the calculation of profit over the asset's life. This process is called depreciation (for tangible assets) and amortization (for intangibles). At the same time, the accountants reduce the figure for the asset in the balance sheet.

Generally, accountants use a really simple method for calculating depreciation: they charge equal amounts to each year. This is called straight-line depreciation. So:

> The cost of a ten-year-life machine is charged 10 per cent each year in the calculation of profit. The charge is called depreciation or amortization. At the end of the first year, the remaining 90 per cent of the cost is still in the balance sheet as the asset.

This assumes that there will be nothing left of the asset at the end of year 10. This might be a reasonable assumption for many machines that a company expects to use until they fall to pieces. It might not be fair for some assets, such as an office building which a company expects to sell after 10 years. The 'life' for depreciation is, of course, the expected life *in the company*, not the life of the asset overall. So, we should take account of any expected residual value if it is big enough to worry about. Accountants would say 'if it is material'.

The proper formula is, then:

$$\text{Depreciation} = \frac{\text{Cost} - \text{Residual Value}}{\text{Life}}$$

Example

Company X bought a building for €200,000 in January 2015. It is expected to have a physical life of 30 years and to be worth zero at the end. Company X expects to sell the building after 15 years for €50,000. Company X also bought the land (on which the building sits) for €1m. It is expected to be sold for €2m in 2030 and to be worth €3m in 2045.

What should be the depreciation expense for these assets in 2015? The answer is:

1. Land. No depreciation, because no limited life.
2. Building. The relevant life is 15 years. The net cost is €200,000 – €50,000. So, the annual expense is €150,000 ÷ 15 = €10,000.

The effect of depreciation on the financial statement is as follows. Suppose that the following two events have occurred: the company set up by the owner putting in €100 of cash, and the company buys a machine for €60 cash. The balance sheet would then appear as follows:

Balance Sheet			
Machine	60	Equity	100
Cash	40		

Suppose that the accountants calculate that the machine will last for ten years, with no residual value, so that the annual depreciation expense is 6. At the end of the first year, the effect is this:

Balance Sheet			
Machine	60	Equity	100
	−6		
	54		
Cash	40		

Income Statement			
Depreciation	6		

You will notice that the balance sheet appears not to add up, but that is because the profit has not yet been calculated. If nothing else at all had happened in the company, the year's loss would be 6, which would be deducted from equity, so both sides would add up to 94.

Sometimes assets suffer nasty accidents

A simple example of an asset losing value is when inventories suffer physical damage or become obsolete. Then, nobody wants to buy them, except at a very low price. Although inventories are usually valued at cost, like most assets, it would not be fair to show them at their full cost if this can never be recovered by selling them. Inventories do not normally wear out over time because an entity hopes to sell them quickly, so accountants do not depreciate them. However, in the case of damage or obsolescence, some immediate recognition of the loss is needed. Accountants (under IFRS) use a simple rule for measurement of inventories: lower of cost or net realizable value.

If we now turn to non-current assets, depreciation takes account of the wear and tear as expected on the date of purchase. However, sometimes there are nasty surprises: the asset catches fire, is stolen, or becomes obsolete more quickly than expected. It would not be fair to ignore this damage. Accountants take account of it by charging an expense and recording a fall in the value of the asset. This is called 'impairment'.

So, if there is an accident, the accountants work out an asset's 'recoverable amount' by asking: what could be got out of the asset by (a) selling it or (b) repairing it and continuing to use it? As long as one of these is higher than the amount recorded for the asset (i.e. the net book value = carrying amount = depreciated cost), there is no problem. If the recoverable amount is lower, then an impairment is recorded by:

- reducing the asset value in the balance sheet and
- charging the amount of the reduction as an expense.

More on intangible assets

We divided assets above into three types by substance (tangible, intangible, and financial); and into two types by time (current and non-current). Intangible assets are especially important in the modern economy. In cities such as London, Hong Kong, or Singapore, labour and land costs are so high that manufacturing industry has been largely driven out. So, in order to be successful, companies need to concentrate on being clever. Investment banks, lawyers, accountancy firms, software houses, and research departments concentrate on using well-trained staff who use and produce intangible items.

The staff themselves are vital ingredients of success, but they are generally not on the balance sheet. Why would trained and loyal staff not be 'assets' of their employing company? The company is probably expecting future benefits from staff, and has had transactions with them in the past. However, staff can resign— often with little notice. Even staff on long contracts are usually allowed or required to go quickly when they resign. So, staff are not 'controlled'. For this reason, they are not treated as assets. This also means that training courses and other costs related to staff are treated as expenses rather than assets.

Intangibles purchased from outside the company are put in the balance sheet. These include patents, licences, and brand names. A common way of buying these is for a company to take over another company. The new company becomes a subsidiary, and the intangibles gained appear in the new combined balance sheet even if they were not in the subsidiary's balance sheet. You might like to look at the intangible assets shown by a real company. For example, pharmaceutical companies generally have substantial amounts of intangibles. You could look at the balance sheet in the annual report of GlaxoSmithKline.

Nevertheless, there are plenty of intangible items missing from balance sheets in pharmaceutical companies, and in other industries such as banking. You would need to take account of this when assessing the value of such companies. Research costs might well meet the definition of asset, but accountants are so unsure about the future benefits that such costs are treated as expenses.

Liabilities

A liability is defined in IFRS as:

- a *present* obligation
- caused by a *past* event
- expected to lead to *future* outflows.

Notice that the liability is not a *future* obligation but one that already exists. The future aspect of the liability is the expected outflow of benefits (usually cash). Liabilities include amounts owed to: the bank, suppliers, tax authorities, and bond holders. However, the following items are *not* liabilities: next year's wages bill, private intentions of the company to spend on restructuring, public intentions of the company to pay dividends, announced before the AGM, and expected operating losses that are probable.

Why do these latter items not meet the definition? The answers are as follows:

1. Next year's wages bill is an expected outflow but there is no present obligation to pay it, because the workers have not yet worked.

2. The intentions of the directors could be reversed later. They do not create an obligation to pay amounts to particular people.

3. Dividends do not become a legal obligation until the shareholders vote for them at the company's annual general meeting (AGM). This is *after* the year end.

4. However likely future operating losses are, there is no obligation to make them or to pay them to someone.

A slightly more complicated version of a liability is a 'provision', defined in IFRS as 'a liability of uncertain timing or amount', as explained here in Box 7.

Box 7

Provisions include

- in Glaxo's balance sheet (which you might have consulted earlier), there is a liability for pension payments to staff

- in BP's balance sheet at the end of 2011, there was a huge provision for cleaning up the oil spill in the Caribbean that happened in 2010.

How do these two provisions meet the definition of a liability?

1. *Pensions.* The past event is the employment contract, followed by the workers doing some work. This creates the obligation to make future payments.

2. *Clean-up.* The past event was causing the oil spill. The law requires a clean-up, and it was already clear that many law cases would probably be lost. So, there is an obligation, with an expected outflow. This sort of provision is called a 'loss contingency' in the USA.

Measuring liabilities

As with assets, once it has been decided to put a liability into a balance sheet, it is then necessary to consider how to measure it. Most liabilities are recorded at how much the company expects to pay. However, there is a problem: sometimes the payment is expected to be years into the future. Should we take account of the fact that a distant liability is not so worrying as one to be paid tomorrow? For such provisions (e.g. the pension and clean-up provisions discussed above), accountants do adjust distant liabilities downwards. This is called 'discounting'. It takes account of the time value of money. If you could get a 10 per cent interest rate on money put into the bank, then $100 put into the bank now would give you $110 in one year's time (or more with compound interest). So, an outflow of $110 in one year's time is equal to an outflow of $100 now.

Income statements

As explained in Chapter 3, the income statement is a measure of success or performance for a period. It shows the income and expenses of the period. The income could include items such as in Box 8.

Financial reports of listed companies

Box 8
- selling inventories for cash
- selling inventories in exchange for cash to be received later
- receipts from renting out a property
- dividends or interest received from investments
- selling non-current assets for more than their accounting value
- an increase in value of shares in other companies or (under IFRS) of investment property.

These types of income are of different qualities. Income statements show them under various different headings. The first, and generally largest, amount is sales or 'revenue'. The basic business model of most companies is to sell inventories for more than they cost to buy or to make. Accountants focus on the selling transaction and ignore any previous rise in value of the inventory. To be on the safe side, the sale transaction is not counted until the inventory is taken by (or delivered to) the customer. This fits with the definition of the asset: it ceases to be the seller's asset when control is passed to the customer by delivery.

However, for some other assets, accountants now also take account of increases in value before sale, particularly for assets whose value is easy to measure, such as shares in listed companies or properties rented out.

Expenses include such things as: the cost of the inventories sold, wages, depreciation and impairment of assets, and a decrease in value of shares or investment property.

You could now look at examples of income statements from a large listed company.

Some of the income and expenses are regarded as so far from cash or so removed from the control of the directors that they are shown separately as 'other comprehensive income' (OCI). Unfortunately, there is no clear principle to explain which these items are, only some complicated rules. Common examples of OCI are: gains and losses caused by exchange rate movements affecting a group's investments in foreign subsidiaries, increases or decreases in the value of certain types of investments, and certain parts of the expense related to pensions for employees.

These OCI items can be large and volatile from one year to the next. Companies are generally happy to be able to show these in a separate statement. The amounts *before* the items of OCI are shown in an income statement which totals to 'profit or loss' or 'earnings'. After OCI has been included, the total is 'comprehensive income'. If you look at any large company's report (using IFRS or US GAAP), you will see these two income statements, often on the same page.

Table 17. Various profit figures

sales
− cost of sales
= gross profit
± other operating revenues/expenses
= operating profit
± financial items (e.g. interest)
= net profit before tax
− tax
= net profit after tax ('earnings')
± other comprehensive income
= comprehensive income

The income statements could be seen as being divided into three types of item: operating, financial, and other. However, there is no clear definition of any of these terms. So, practice varies somewhat between companies. In more detail, various calculations of profit (gross, net, and so on) are presented in the income statements, as shown in Table 17.

As explained in Chapter 1, this book does not cover taxation. However, a brief note about the taxation of corporate income is needed here. In most countries, taxation works company-by-company, rather than group-by-group. That is, each individual legal entity is taxed on profits in its own country of registration, using the accounting and tax rules of that country. In some countries (e.g. Germany), the accounting and tax rules are fairly close. For some companies in such countries, the 'taxable income' is exactly the same thing as the 'net profit before tax'. However, in other countries (e.g. the USA and the

UK), the tax authorities require many adjustments to be made to the accounting numbers in order to calculate taxable income. For example, if an investment property is revalued upwards to fair value (in a UK GAAP or IFRS balance sheet), the resulting gain is recorded for accounting but ignored for taxation until the property is sold. Accountants then treat the tax that would be paid on the gain if the asset had been sold as a sort of postponed tax, called a 'deferred tax liability'.

Interpretation: accounting ratios

You might assume that a company's financial strength can be measured by the size of its assets or sales, or perhaps more importantly by the profits. However, looking at an individual figure on its own, such as the sales or profit, can be misleading. By deriving certain accounting ratios we are better able to evaluate the financial status of a business.

Suppose that there are two companies: A and B. Their respective net profits are $20,000 and $50,000. From this you might conclude that company B is the more profitable of the two. However, let us now introduce some additional information:

	Co. A ($)	Co. B ($)
Net profit	20,000	50,000
Sales	160,000	500,000

Now which of the two companies is the more profitable—is it still company B?

Another way of looking at the profitability of a business is to create a ratio, putting the net profit over the sales figure and expressing it as a percentage (× 100):

$$\frac{20,000}{160,000} \times 100 \qquad\qquad \frac{50,000}{500,000} \times 100$$

= 12.5% = 10%

This emphasizes that looking at net profit on its own can be misleading. If we put net profit into context with some other information, such as sales in the above example, we can deduce more meaningful information about the firm.

Let us examine another ratio for two other companies:

	Co. C ($)	Co. D ($)
Net profit	60,000	60,000
Financed by	500,000	250,000

Looking only at net profit, both companies are the same. As before, this view can change as we add information. If we create a ratio, this time net profit over 'financed by' (the long-term debt and equity), we find the following results:

$$\frac{60,000}{500,000} \times 100 \qquad\qquad \frac{60,000}{250,000} \times 100$$

= 12% = 24%

Now we see that company D is the more profitable even though both companies generated the same amount of net profits.

Liquidity

A liquidity ratio assesses whether a firm can meet its current obligations from its current assets. That is, can the company pay off its debts as they arise in the short-term?

$$\text{a)} \quad \text{Current ratio} \quad = \quad \frac{\text{Current assets}}{\text{Current liabilities}}$$

There is no particular good or bad size for this ratio. It depends on which type of industry the company is in. However, a danger signal would be if the ratio is falling, or if it is much lower than that of other companies in the same industry.

Financial (capital) structure

A financial structure ratio measures how much the firm is funded by equity capital and how much by debt capital, in other words, what proportion of the funds comes from the owners and what proportion from outside lenders (such as the banks). This ratio is known as 'gearing' or 'leverage'. If a company is highly geared, this implies that the business is funded by a lot of debt. High gearing means that the owners will benefit when profits rise, because the lenders will still only receive their fixed return.

Gearing also measures risk. Low-geared companies are low risk and vice versa. Large loans mean more interest charges, which must be paid irrespective of how profitable the year has been. So, high gearing can make a company very vulnerable. Interest has to be paid, as does the eventual loan repayment.

The ratios in this category are expressed as a percentage, so we multiply by 100 (percent).

$$\text{Gearing} = \frac{\text{Long-term loans}}{\text{Shareholders' funds} + \text{Long-term loans}} \times 100$$

Note that this is only one variation of the gearing ratio. It would also be possible to measure loans compared to equity. As usual, the key theme is that, once you have chosen a version, keep to that ratio consistently across time and across companies.

Earnings per share (EPS)

The 'earnings per share' ratio is often abbreviated to 'EPS'. Assuming that the company has only issued ordinary shares, the formula is:

$$\text{EPS} = \frac{\text{Net profit after tax}}{\text{Number of shares issued}}$$

The ratio is expressed as cents or pence per share. For the unusual companies which have also issued preference shares, the denominator remains the number of ordinary shares, but any preference dividends are deducted from the profit in the numerator because the company is obliged to pay them before paying dividends to the ordinary shareholders. The EPS ratio measures the amount of profit earned for each ordinary share.

It is very unlikely that the board of directors would wish to give out all the retained profits to the shareholders; instead, they are likely to suggest retaining some profits for internal growth, acquisitions, and so on. So what the shareholders will receive as cash dividends is usually less than the EPS.

Price earnings ratio (p/e ratio)

The ratio of the share price to the earnings is often abbreviated to 'the p/e ratio'.

$$\text{p/e} = \frac{\text{Market price per share}}{\text{Earnings per share}}$$

This ratio compares the current market price of the company's shares with the earnings generated. It indicates the 'expensiveness' of the share. Another way of looking at this ratio is that it shows the confidence level of investors. A high p/e ratio indicates a high level of confidence in the company; in other words, the market is prepared to pay a high price for a share in the company, compared to its earnings. This is because the market expects a good future for the company. Many newspapers report daily on the p/e ratios of listed companies.

Misleading accounts

Accounting numbers and ratios are used for many purposes. It is inevitable that the preparers of the numbers (e.g. the management of large companies) will try to make them look as good as possible. For example, a company might: hide liabilities or invent assets so that it looks safer; or exaggerate sales or understate expenses so that it looks more profitable. Looking more profitable would be especially useful if the company is trying to raise more money from the public or if the directors' bonuses depend on the size of profit. The various tricks that managers might play are summarized here in Box 9.

Box 9
- *window dressing:* engaging in transactions designed temporarily to improve the appearance of the company—for example, selling non-current assets to get cash just before the year end
- *creative accounting:* stretching the accounting rules by spotting loopholes or by exploiting a lack of clarity
- *off-balance-sheet finance:* incurring obligations which are not recorded as liabilities—for example, by signing short leases or by incurring the liabilities in entities that are designed to fall outside of the definition of subsidiary.

Of course, it would be possible for directors to just break the rules and present plain lies. There are mechanisms that are designed to stop all this (or ensure disclosure of it), as examined in Chapter 6. However, sometimes the mechanisms do not work. There have been spectacular examples, as seen in Box 10.

Box 10

- in the late 1920s in the USA, before the Wall Street Crash, many companies invented assets or valued them wildly

- in 2001, Enron (a vast US energy-trading company) collapsed after recording gains based on the doubtful market values of financial contracts, and hiding liabilities in off-balance-sheet 'special purpose vehicles'

- in 2003, when the Italian dairy company Parmalat collapsed, it was found that €4 billion of cash assumed to be in a bank account did not exist and that the debts of €14 billion were eight times larger than previously published.

To extend the continuum of ability to mislead (attributed to Disraeli), there are lies, damned lies, statistics, and financial statements. However, that does not mean that statistics and financial statements cannot be useful. It means that they must be interpreted carefully.

Other disclosures

A company's annual report also contains other types of information. The report of the president/chair person reviews the year and looks ahead. Readers might be able to detect useful signals about expected performance of the company. The directors' report contains many factors, some required by regulations. Annual reports now contain information about the company's use of resources. This can be seen under the headings of 'carbon accounting' or 'sustainability accounting'.

Chapter 5
International differences and standardization

Among other things, this chapter addresses the following questions: Just how different can accounting numbers be for the same company under different accounting rules? Which countries use International Financial Reporting Standards (IFRS)? In what main ways is US 'generally accepted accounting principles' (US GAAP) different from IFRS? How have politics and economics affected accounting?

International differences

International standardization of financial reporting by listed companies is useful because many companies and investors operate internationally, and there are great international differences in how accounting is done. International standardization simplifies the preparation of financial statements covering whole international groups, and it improves the comparability of the accounting information, for managers and investors. An indication of the scale of international difference can be seen in those cases where companies publish two sets of accounting figures based on different rules. Comparisons of accounting under domestic rules with that under US rules were commonly published by foreign companies that were listed on US stock exchanges. Table 18 shows some interesting examples for earnings. Daimler-Benz was the first German company to provide

Table 18. Reconciliations of earnings

		Domestic (million)	US-Adjusted (million)	Difference (%)
Daimler-Benz:	1992	DM615	DM(1.839)	-399
	1995	DM(5.734)	DM(5.729)	+1
British Airways:	2003	£72	£(128)	-278
	2006	£451	£148	-67

Source: Author's own work based on published company financial statements

this data, in 1993. The large differences (and the variation from year to year) between German and US profit figures were a surprise to many accountants and users of financial statements.

The figures for British Airways, too, show that profits can need adjustment either up or down. The supply of these interesting reconciliations to US accounting dried up after 2006 because the US authorities accepted IFRS accounting without reconciliation from 2007.

The introduction of IFRS for consolidated statements in many countries in 2005 produced a large number of comparisons of the 2004 balance sheets and profits: (i) as published under the previous national system in 2004, and (ii) as republished as comparative figures under IFRS in 2005. For Canadian companies, the exercise was performed for 2010 in 2011.

These large differences are created by the sort of topics discussed earlier in this book: depreciation methods, impairment calculations, the valuation of inventories, and so on. Indeed, since the differences shown in Table 18 are earnings and net assets, they might hide much larger differences on particular accounting topics that happen to cancel out.

The basic reason for international differences in accounting is that the main purpose of accounting has varied by country and over time. For example, by the last quarter of the twentieth century, the purpose for listed companies in the USA was to give useful information to investors to help them to predict cash flows in order to make economic decisions. By contrast, the purpose for most German companies was to calculate taxable income and prudently distributable profit.

Fairly recently, a useful compromise has been reached in many countries. For example, German-listed companies use IFRS for the consolidated statements sent to investors, but all German companies use German GAAP in the unconsolidated statements used for tax and dividend decisions.

IFRS

IFRS are issued by the International Accounting Standards Board (IASB), which is an independent private-sector trust. Its predecessor, the International Accounting Standards Committee (IASC) began work in 1973, as shown by the title page of the 'Agreement' between accountancy bodies of nine countries, which set up the IASC (see Figure 10). Both bodies were/are based in London, with English as the operating language.

IFRS is required for the consolidated statements of listed companies in the EU. The same applies in Australia, Canada, Hong Kong, New Zealand, South Africa, and several other countries. In China, listed companies use a set of Chinese accounting standards based approximately on IFRS. In Japan and Switzerland, IFRS is allowed but not required.

The IASB adopted all the IASC's standards (called IASs). For most accounting topics, there is a standard. Some examples of standards (and their requirements) on issues that we have dealt with in earlier chapters are shown in Table 19.

Some differences between IFRS and US GAAP

Most listed companies in the world are now using either IFRS or US GAAP. We have sometimes noted the difference in terminology between US reporting and typical IFRS reporting. Here, we look at two differences between US GAAP and IFRS: US GAAP is more detailed and tends to be written in terms of rules rather than principles; and, related to this, US GAAP has fewer options than IFRS.

AN AGREEMENT

to establish an
International
Accounting Standards
Committee

London
Friday 29th June 1973

10. The front page of the founding document of the IASC

Table 19. Examples of IFRS standards (and their requirements)

Old standards still in operation

IAS 1	Presentation of financial statements (financial statements should give a fair presentation)
IAS 2	Inventories (measure inventories at the lower of cost and net realizable value)
IAS 7	Cash flow statements (statements should show operating, investing and financing flows)
IAS 16	Property, plant, and equipment (PPE should be depreciated if it has a limited useful life)
IAS 38	Intangible assets (development costs should be shown as assets if they meet certain criteria)
IAS 39	Financial instruments (traded marketable securities should be measured at fair value)

New standards

IFRS 3	Business combinations (goodwill should not be amortized but annually tested for impairment)
IFRS 10	Consolidated financial statements (a subsidiary is an entity controlled by another entity)

An example of a rule compared to a principle is the definition of subsidiary. In IFRS, a subsidiary is defined in terms of control, which is the power to affect the returns coming from another entity. This is a little vague. Sometimes it is not exactly clear whether that power exists. US GAAP prefers generally to restrict consolidation to entities in which another company owns more than half the voting shares. That is easier to audit but can leave controlled entities out of the consolidation.

Three examples of options in IFRS but not US GAAP are as follows. First, balance sheets can start with cash, as in the USA, but can also use an order of assets that ends with cash. Second, in the cash flow statement (see Chapter 3), IFRS allows interest paid to be shown as a financing cash outflow rather than as an operating outflow (as required in the USA), which might make the net operating inflow look much better. Third, land and buildings can be measured at fair value rather than on a cost basis, which can make assets look much more valuable.

There is one major reverse example—in other words, where US GAAP has an extra choice: IFRS does not allow last-in first-out (LIFO) for inventory measurement whereas it is common in US GAAP statements. LIFO means that the accountants assume that the last (most recent) inventories bought are the first ones to be used up. This is unlikely to be a good way actually to manage inventories, but the LIFO assumption has nothing necessarily to do with reality, it is just an accounting method.

Why LIFO matters

Suppose that the price of a particular inventory tends to rise over time. What effects on the balance sheet and the profit will be caused if the accountants assume LIFO rather than first-in

Have a look at the note on inventories on page A-12 of the report of the US company Caterpillar Inc at <http://www.caterpillar.com/investors/financial-information/sec-filings>. Go to 'annual forms', then Form '10-K' for 2012. You will see the size of the LIFO: the FIFO number would have been $2.4 billion higher. Then look at the balance sheet on page A-6. If FIFO had been used, what percentage effect would there be on net assets (which is equal to stockholders' equity)? You can calculate this as an increase of 18.7 per cent. This would be the size of the effect on the ratios of gearing or profit, as examined in Chapter 4.

first-out (FIFO)? The answer is that it would make the balance sheet look worse (older, cheaper inventory) and the profit worse (using up newer, dearer inventories in the calculation of profit). Why might a company want those effects? One possibility is that, if the tax calculation is tied to the income statement, then a lower profit will be useful.

Politics and accounting

Accounting is, of course, absolutely central to the world of business and it operates in the context of law. However, it is not cut off from the wider world of politics or economics, as shown by the following examples in Box 11.

Box 11

- the collapse of the City of Glasgow Bank in 1878 led to compulsory audit for banks and then other UK companies

- the more general collapse of the US stock market and then the economy led to the creation of the Securities and Exchange Commission, which still regulates financial reporting and auditing of listed companies

- the UK joining the EU (as it now is) in 1973 was the main spur to the setting up by accountants of the IASC to try to keep accounting out of the control of governments

- the re-unification of Germany after the fall of the Berlin Wall in 1989 led to a great expansion of German companies and a search for capital in New York and London, which led to the adoption of international standards in Germany

- the EU had always been opposed to the IASC, as a Trojan horse of Anglo-American accounting, but eventually it accepted IFRS as the only practical way of getting harmonized standards for EU capital markets

- the collapse of Enron and Arthur Andersen in 2001 onwards led to a major increase in US regulation (the Sarbanes-Oxley Act) which made London more attractive than New York as a financial centre, and further strengthened IFRS

- the inability of governments in Roman law countries (e.g. France) to give up control of accounting has led to constant attempts at political interference from the EU in the operations of the IASB. For example, under political pressure, the IASB changed IAS 39 (on financial instruments) in 2008.

Chapter 6
Regulation and audit

In this chapter, we examine some aspects of the regulation of financial reporting, addressing such questions as: Why was the UK the first country to require published audited financial statements from companies? What sort of regulation does the state impose on accounting? Why does the USA have the world's oldest and toughest regulator of financial reporting? What is the purpose of audit? Does it really work? How is an audit conducted?

Although there are 'international standards' for financial reporting, the International Accounting Standards Board (IASB) has no power to impose them on companies. So, the rules are imposed within a national legal system. The same applies to auditing and to other mechanisms for monitoring and enforcement of the rules. This chapter begins with two national examples of regulatory frameworks: the UK and the USA. The UK's requirements for financial reporting and auditing have the longest history in the world. The USA has the world's largest stock markets, the oldest stock-market regulator, and the only really important national standard-setter.

One of the distinguishing features of the UK and the USA (compared to France, Germany, or Japan, for example) is the greater age, size, and importance of the accountancy profession. There are far more auditors per head of population in English-speaking countries than elsewhere. This chapter looks at the nature of auditing and the accountancy profession.

The UK regulatory framework

The UK was the first country to experience the industrial revolution, therefore to need large companies, therefore to need many investors/shareholders, and therefore to need limited liability companies. Limited companies were first formed in large numbers in the UK in the middle of the nineteenth century. Their great merit is to provide a means for the owners of companies to limit the risks associated with participation in a business, and yet to enjoy the rewards of doing so. This may seem an unreasonably fortunate position for the shareholders, but there are many reasons why the existence of such limited liability companies is to the general advantage of the economy. First, many business ventures necessarily involve high risk, particularly in new markets. Without the advantage of limited liability, owner-managers may be deterred from taking the risks necessary in an enterprise culture. As businesses grow, they may require more finance than can be raised from their original owners/managers. In order to attract finance from investors who will not participate in the running of the company, shares can be offered in exchange for money, with the risk limited to the amount invested. This contrasts with the position of most partnerships where each partner is personally liable without limit for the liabilities incurred by the partnership.

Naturally, investors who will have no active part in the management of the company, and may not even know those who are running it, deserve some protection from unscrupulous and incompetent managers. In addition to limited liability, some other protection is granted by law. An important safeguard is the right to receive financial statements from the directors showing the profit of the company and its state of affairs, together with quite a lot of detailed information as required by various regulations.

Companies Acts, containing some reporting requirements, were passed in the UK from 1844 onwards. Examples of what the 2006 Act now requires are seen here in Box 12.

Box 12
- companies to keep accounting records
- directors to prepare annual financial statements
- auditors to be appointed, except for certain small private companies
- annual reports (including the financial statements) to be sent to the shareholders and made public by sending them to a government official (the Registrar of Companies)
- the company to hold an annual general meeting (AGM) of shareholders, at which directors and auditors are appointed and dividends are voted on.

The Companies Act contains some accounting instructions, which mostly come from 'Directives' from the European Union. However, the detail of UK 'generally accepted accounting principles' (GAAP) is found in accounting standards that are issued by a private sector independent trust: the Financial Reporting Council. UK GAAP is the normal basis of accounting for unlisted companies, although such companies are allowed to use IFRS instead. However, for the consolidated statements of listed companies, there is no choice: IFRS must be used because an EU regulation requires it. Strictly speaking, it is 'IFRS as adopted in the EU' that is required, but the differences between that and IFRS need not concern us in this book.

Compliance with the accounting rules is monitored by another private sector body, the Financial Reporting Review Panel, which is allowed to take companies to court for 'defective accounts'. Court cases seldom happen but the threat of them (and the resulting bad publicity for a company) is a powerful incentive for companies and auditors to report properly.

The US regulatory framework

In the USA, much regulation operates at the state level. Most states have no accounting or audit requirements. So, most companies have no need to appoint auditors or to publish financial statements. However, after the Wall Street Crash of 1929, Congress passed Securities Acts that brought into being the

11. **Crowds gather in Wall Street in October 1929**

Securities and Exchange Commission (SEC) which is the world's oldest and toughest regulator of stock markets. Figure 11 shows an aspect of the chaos of October 1929 in the USA.

The SEC is only interested in listed companies and only in their consolidated statements. For such statements, the SEC requires the company to appoint auditors and to make very extensive disclosures. The SEC could write the detailed rules of US GAAP but has normally allowed private sector standard-setters to do that. From 1973, the approved body for this has been the Financial Accounting Standards Board (FASB), which writes US GAAP. The SEC monitors and enforces the use of GAAP by companies.

Up to (and including) 2006, foreign companies that were listed on US exchanges had to use US GAAP or numerically explain any differences from US GAAP. From 2007, the SEC accepts IFRS from foreigners. For over a decade now, there has been a slow process of removing the differences between IFRS and US GAAP, as mentioned in Chapter 5.

Background to auditing

In Chapter 1, Table 1 shows the age and size of some accountancy bodies. The oldest bodies are in the UK, because the UK first had large numbers of auditors because it first had large numbers of limited companies whose owners and managers were not the same people. The basic role of an auditor is to report on financial information produced by a company's directors, in order to give it greater credibility. A large part of the work of most accounting firms now consists in auditing or similar reporting work, although the UK accountancy profession has even earlier roots in liquidation and insolvency work.

It is clear that shareholders need to be able to rely upon this information with confidence. For this reason, the law (since 1900 in the UK) requires that the reports of many limited companies be audited by suitably qualified independent accountants. In countries which have no such general requirement for audit, it is usually only listed companies which have to appoint auditors. For example, this is required by the SEC in the USA.

It is not only the shareholders who are interested in reliable financial information. There are other types of investors—for example, bondholders who have lent the company money. Then there are other interested parties who are not investors. For example, a bank that intends to lend money to a limited company will wish to know that the financial statements to be used as one means of assessing the financial strength of the borrower have been properly prepared. Likewise, creditors (those who supply goods and services to a company and will be paid in the future for them), will often wish to examine the financial statements of a company before granting credit to it. If a company fails and goes into liquidation, the lenders/creditors will not in general be able to extract additional money from the shareholders above their original capital contribution. It is therefore right that, if they examine the financial statements of what seems to be a profitable company, they should have some assurance, through the auditor's report, that the statements are reliable. There is nothing like the onset of financial difficulties to place almost irresistible pressure upon the directors of a company to show a position more favourable than is really the case. It is the auditors' responsibility to try to stop this happening, or to qualify their audit report if it does. Especially for large companies, the parties interested in financial reports extend further still, beyond those with a direct interest in the company, to governments and the public.

Given that most important companies operate on a multinational basis, the auditors also have to do so. For example, the giant pharmaceutical company, GlaxoSmithKline, is based in London, listed in London and New York, and operates in dozens of countries. For the purposes of UK law and the London stock exchange, it produces IFRS consolidated financial statements for its worldwide operations, as though the group were a single entity using the same accounting rules everywhere. The statements are audited by PwC, in the context of UK law and auditing requirements. The same set of financial statements, but a different audit report, is used for the New York stock exchange. Then all the component parts of the group (the parent and all the subsidiaries) produce individual reports for local purposes, such as taxation, using local accounting rules. Some of these reports are audited and published, depending on the national requirements where the subsidiaries are based.

Many other organizations (such as hospitals or universities) have their financial statements audited, often because this is required by law or by their constitutions. It adds to the credibility of their financial reports and hence to their stewardship.

Auditors

Not every accountant is allowed to be a company auditor. In the UK, for example, the law recognizes the members of some bodies (e.g. the various institutes of accountants, see Chapter 1). In the USA, the SEC is in charge of approving auditors of listed companies.

Duties and responsibilities

The principal duty of the auditor is to report upon the financial statements prepared by the directors. Note that the auditor is not in charge of preparing the statements, and cannot force the directors to change them. The culmination of the audit process is the publication of an 'opinion' on whether the financial statements give a 'true and fair view' (UK) or 'fair presentation' (USA) of the company's cash flows, financial position and profit or loss, in the context of the prevailing law and accounting rules. The audit report can usually be found immediately before the financial statements, often about half-way through a company's annual report.

The idea of 'fairness' reflects the fact that accounting is not an exact science and that there may be a number of different ways in which to present broadly similar information. The term conveys the idea that the financial statements have been honestly prepared to reflect the facts, and are not misleading to readers.

It is now most unusual to see an audit report of a listed company which gives an opinion that the financial statements are not fair. It would trigger an investigation by the regulators, such as the SEC in the USA or the Review Panel in the UK. This means that the auditors have considerable persuasive power over the directors. However, it is common for auditors to include comments in their report or to draw attention to particular points in the financial statements.

Independence

The principal function of the audit is to add credibility to the documents published by the directors of a company. It is therefore of fundamental importance that the auditor should have no personal interest in the success of the company. No rule can guarantee independence and objectivity; they are personal qualities required of an auditor. Nevertheless, in most countries, the law prevents an auditor from being a director or an employee of a company (his or her client) of which he or she is an auditor, and the rules of the professional bodies further prohibit him or her from holding shares in it. Additionally, accountancy firms have their own rules to ensure that their partners and staff are seen to be as independent as possible. Thus, a student who owns some shares may find on joining an accountancy firm that he or she has to sell them to comply with the firm's independence rules.

Another way of putting this is that the auditor is required to exercise 'professional scepticism', that is to be alert for any examples of misleading accounting. The auditor should be constantly alert to the possibility that the employees of the client are attempting to hide liabilities, invent profits, and so on.

It is paradoxical that, although the audit firm is legally appointed by and responsible to the shareholders, and is required to report independently upon the statements produced by the directors, it will often owe its appointment to a proposal made by the directors to the shareholders. All this can place considerable obstacles in the path of an auditor's independence, but there are safeguards in law to protect the auditor who may have to thwart the directors' intentions. Especially in the USA, auditors are sometimes sued by creditors and others when a company collapses. This is a further incentive to do their work properly.

However, there have certainly been cases where the auditors have got too close to the directors, partly because of all the non-audit work granted by the directors. In practice, the auditor often sees the audited company (rather than its shareholders) as 'the client'. The most spectacular example was the collapse of the US energy-trading company Enron in 2001, which then led to the demise of the formerly highly-regarded audit firm Arthur Andersen.

The quality of independence must be accompanied by the strength of character necessary to follow it through. In difficult situations, the auditor will often find him- or herself in conflict with the management of his or her client's (the shareholders') company, and it is in these circumstances that true worth is tested.

What is an audit?

The four stages of an audit are: (i) accepting and defining the terms of the engagement, (ii) planning, including the assessment of risk and the level of materiality, (iii) gathering evidence, and (iv) reporting to the client and others. If financial statements are to give a fair view, they must reflect the business transactions of the company. To take the example of the sales of a company, the questions which the auditor will ask include those in Box 13.

Box 13

- Have all sales been recorded?

- Did all the recorded sales actually take place?

- Are all the sales those of the company itself?

- Have the sales been recorded at the correct amount?

- Have the sales been recorded in the correct period?

- If sales have been made on credit and the corresponding amounts have not been received, will they be fully recovered?

- Have the sales and receivables been properly presented in the financial statements?

Some of the key aspects of audit are examined in the rest of this section.

Materiality

The auditor is, of course, not concerned to see that every small sale has been recorded. The reader of the income statement of a company with total sales of approximately €1,000m would probably not consider it important if those sales had actually been €1m more or less than shown. The auditor must consider *materiality* and must decide what size of error or misstatement is likely to be material to a proper understanding. Once he or she has decided what is likely to be material, the auditor will carry out such work as will enable him or her to be satisfied that the statements are not likely to be materially misstated. Certainty could only be achieved by an exhaustive examination of all transactions undertaken by a company, and it is doubtful whether absolute certainty could ever be achieved even in relation to the smallest of companies, let alone a large one. An auditor therefore has two very important judgements to make, right at the start of his or her work: what is going to be material to this client, and what work is needed for the necessary level of assurance to express the 'opinion'? These are only the first of many judgements.

Forming a view

The first stage of answering the above questions is to have a thorough understanding of the client's business, without which no view can be formed about whether the financial statements reflect the client's economic activity. The next stage is to consider the client's accounting systems. If they look likely to produce accurate information, then the auditor may be able to carry out less work in substantiating final figures. This will be possible if the client has a good system of *internal control.*

Internal control is the means by which the directors of a company ensure that the accounting systems produce accurate information, and that the assets and liabilities of the company are properly recorded and, in the case of assets, adequately safeguarded. If the directors attach importance to internal control then this attitude is likely to pervade the company, and the accounting systems are likely to produce accurate information. However, the auditor must always be alert for flaws in the system which could negate other satisfactory controls.

The examination of the accounting systems and internal controls also gives the auditors an opportunity to provide a service to the client. Their experience of many businesses, and of the sorts of things that can go wrong in accounting systems, makes them particularly well placed to give guidance and advice to clients. Although this is not part of their statutory duties, good auditors see this as a service they can provide to their clients as a direct consequence of the work they must do in any event.

Armed with knowledge of the business and an understanding of the accounting control systems, the auditor will decide how to approach the work on the financial statements themselves. If the control systems seem satisfactory, the auditor can rely upon them for some assurance that the accounting information (which is the end product of the system) is reasonably accurate. If he or she intends to do this, he or she must make a further examination of the controls to see that they are indeed operating in a satisfactory way. Alternatively, the auditor may conclude that the control systems are not reliable or that it is more efficient to go straight to a more detailed examination of the information that is generated. The auditor will always carry out some testing, verification, and analysis of the information contained in the statements, although this will be less in those cases where reliance can be placed on the system of internal control.

This ability sometimes to rely on the system of internal control, together with the application of statistics to the problems of sampling from large masses of information, has taken a lot of the routine out of audit work. Auditors no longer examine large numbers of transactions, but now use their skills of analysis to reduce the need for this work.

Computers

The importance of computers to the auditor is now very great. Virtually all businesses make use of some form of computing as part of their accounting and management information systems. At the very least, the auditor must have an understanding of the nature of computer systems and the problems, particularly of control, associated with them. Indeed, the use of sophisticated techniques of analysis and interrogation of IT systems is now an important part of an auditor's work.

Questions of judgement

Towards the end of the audit work, there may be difficult questions of judgement on matters of valuation and presentation. The senior members of the auditing firm will spend much of their time on these. For example, a company may wish to carry forward the costs of development of a new product as an asset on its balance sheet. The IFRS accounting rules require this to be done, but only under defined circumstances. For example, the cost associated with the project must be identifiable, and the ultimate revenues must be expected to exceed the cost of development.

These will be difficult questions for an outsider to decide upon, but the auditor must make appropriate enquiries and form a judgement. It is on such matters that the views of an auditor will most often diverge from those of the directors of the client. The auditor must necessarily approach the problem with some scepticism, while the directors, who instigated and approved the project, may be reluctant to admit that their decisions are not going to bear fruit.

Another frequent source of difference between auditors and directors is the question of the valuation of inventories. As noted in Chapter 4, the general rule is that inventory is included in a company's balance sheet as an asset at the lower of its cost and its *net realizable value*. In some cases, even the cost of inventory can be difficult to determine, especially if it has been made by the company itself: careful record keeping will be necessary and some judgement may be involved in making allocations of costs to specific items. However, the net realizable value of inventory may be even more difficult to determine, particularly if it is slow moving or relates to obsolete models. For example, a car manufacturer may have to keep stocks of parts for models which have been discontinued; as time passes, sales of these parts will diminish and difficult judgements will have to be made on whether all the parts held by the company will be sold. Again, this is an area where the views of auditors and managements often diverge.

In times of economic difficulty, such as have been experienced in much of the world from 2008, another key judgement relates to whether or not the business is a going concern. If it seems not to be, the company or the auditor should report the problem, which will affect the way that assets are valued. Naturally, the directors will try to resist this eventuality. Even without generally difficult times, the march of innovation leaves some businesses behind, such as the high-street retailers who are struggling to survive the onset of e-commerce.

Fraud

A difficult area for the auditor is the question of fraud. In the popular mind, the detection and prevention of fraud is one of the auditor's primary aims. However, auditors themselves take a contrary view, and this is an example of an 'expectations gap' between the auditors' actual task and what the public or the newspapers think it is. Nevertheless, auditors certainly plan their work to have a reasonable expectation of finding material errors that will affect the financial statements. Many such errors will be unintentional, but from time to time they may be caused by fraud. Every auditor would hope, but cannot be certain, that the audit will detect material fraud. Unfortunately, because of the possibility of collusion and cover-up, it is less likely that the auditor will detect fraud than an equally material mistake. However, many frauds are not large enough to affect whether or not a fair view is given by the financial statements. The auditor cannot hope to detect or prevent all small frauds. It would be prohibitively expensive. The mere existence of an audit should have a deterrent effect since there is always the chance that fraud will be detected.

If fraud by junior employees is discovered, it is obvious that this can be reported to the senior staff. However, really large frauds might involve the senior accountants or other executives. Fortunately, nearly all listed companies have audit committees (see next sub-section), so the auditors can report problems to those committees. Assuming that, despite any fraud, the financial statements comply with the rules and give a fair presentation, there will be no external reporting of fraud or its detection.

Some rules for auditors

Auditors operate within the framework of company law. In the UK, for example, certain companies (including all listed companies) must appoint auditors, whose prime duty is to give an opinion on whether the financial statements prepared by the directors give a true and fair view. The law also restricts who may be appointed as an auditor, and limits the term of the auditor's appointment.

Just as there are 'standards' for financial reporting so there are auditing standards on many of the issues discussed in this section. As for financial reporting, national standards have now largely been replaced by 'International Standards on Auditing' which are written by committees of accountants, and imposed by national regulations.

There are also codes of corporate governance, designed for listed companies, requiring the appointment of an audit committee, which contains independent directors.

A mix of work for accountants

As explained in Chapter 1, the accountancy firms do many types of work in addition to auditing, such as insolvency, tax, and consultancy. The parts of the firms that deal with auditing (or more generally 'assurance') have a rather seasonal flow of work. This is because, within many countries, most companies' accounting year-ends are the same: in the USA or Germany, this is 31 December; in Japan, 31 March; and in Australia, 30 June. This means that there are particularly busy times of the year, generally starting a few weeks after the year end. However, many listed companies are required to publish quarterly or half-yearly reports, which require some audit attention, and much of the background work can go on all year round. For example, the auditors of a huge company such as Shell work there all year.

Furthermore, accountants with an auditing or investigation background will often be asked to carry out other work that requires an independent opinion to be expressed. This may include reporting on claims for financial assistance (e.g. claims by companies for grants awarded by government departments in certain circumstances); or upon financial statements which are to form the basis of cost-sharing or profit-sharing. For example, reports may be required upon the operations of a North Sea oil rig which is operated by one company, but in which a number of companies have a financial interest.

Accountants may be asked to participate in government enquiries. For example, there is a well-established procedure under UK company law whereby a government ministry appoints inspectors to investigate the affairs of a company. For such enquiries, two inspectors are normally appointed, one a prominent accountant and the other a prominent lawyer. Their complementary talents permit them to establish facts through the analysis of information, in particular accounting information, and the examination of witnesses under oath.

Accountants may also be brought into the resolution of disputes. They may do this as experts or as arbitrators, but in either case, the aim of the parties will be to find an independent person whose opinions can be trusted. The 'expert' is hired by one of the parties to a dispute but needs to be able to persuade the court or tribunal. The 'arbitrator' listens to the arguments of both sides and makes a determination on which they agree to be bound.

Chapter 7

Internal decision-making: costs and volumes

The scope of management accounting

Readers will remember from Chapter 1 that accounting can be
split into two main areas: financial accounting and management
accounting. The final two chapters examine aspects of
management accounting: decision-making and control. Among
other things, this chapter addresses the following questions: What
sort of decisions can management accounting help with? Why are
some costs relevant and others irrelevant? How does a company
decide at what volume to operate? What are indirect costs, and
how are they taken into account in decisions? Let us first recap
the differences between financial and management accounting.

Financial accounting

This is the provision of financial information to outside parties
(external users) such as shareholders or bankers. The information
is designed to make managers accountable to owners, and to assist
investors with economic decisions. Typical financial documents
produced under this category are: the income statement, the
balance sheet, and the cash flow statement. The key points are
that such statements are:

- required by law
- designed for readers outside the organization

- in a prescribed form (laid out following many requirements)
- audited, at least for listed companies
- based on past activities (what a company did in its last accounting period).

Management accounting

This is the provision of financial information to the managers of the firm (internal users). The information is designed to assist managers with internal decisions and to help them control organizations. Typical financial documents produced under this category are: costing reports, break-even reports, and budgets (e.g. cash budgets). The key points are that such documents are:

- prepared frequently and can be very detailed
- not required by law
- designed for readers inside the organization
- not in any prescribed particular form (depends upon what suits each organization)
- based on past, present, and future activities.

There is an overlap between the two areas of accounting, financial and management. Both are based on the collection of financial information, normally through double-entry bookkeeping as examined in Chapters 2 and 3. This chapter looks at decision-making by managers. It examines types of cost and how cost information is used for break-even analysis. Chapter 8 looks at how accounting is used for control, including budgeting and standard costs. Many accountants work inside companies on these very useful tasks of management accounting. As usual, these chapters can only be an introduction to a vast field.

What is meant by cost?

The word 'cost' has many possible meanings. Those relevant for accounting are now examined.

Historical and relevant costs

Historical costs are the amounts actually spent by the entity. They are used for drawing up a set of financial statements. However, the relevant costs for decision-making are different; it is necessary to assess the economic or opportunity cost involved. Suppose that the decision is whether or not an entity should sell a building. The opportunity cost is the amount of money that the entity would forgo (in various ways, e.g. having to rent a replacement building) if it sold the building. The historical cost of the asset in this circumstance is always irrelevant. In other words, when making decisions about future activities, it is future-relevant amounts and not historical costs that matter.

Opportunity costs

Opportunity costs are incurred because, in many cases, making one choice means forgoing the opportunity of other choices. In other words, an opportunity cost can be defined as the value, usually expressed in monetary terms, of being deprived of the next best opportunity as a result of taking a particular decision.

Example of relevant labour costs

One of the costs of deciding to do, or not to do, a project might be labour costs. To decide which labour costs are relevant for the decision, the accountant needs to work out which of the three cases in Box 14 applies to the project.

Box 14

- Labour cost is *irrelevant* if staff would otherwise be doing nothing if they were not working on the project, assuming that the staff would not be laid off by the company (perhaps because an upturn is expected soon, and labour with such skills is in short supply).

- If staff are already fully occupied on other jobs and no more suitable staff can be found quickly, the relevant cost of labour is the loss of the opportunity to do other work for which customers would pay a given amount. In this case, the managers have to make a choice about how to use the resource. If the choice is to transfer labour from one task to another, this implies forgoing the value of the first task in pursuing the alternative.

- If staff are fully occupied but it would be easy to hire more suitable staff quickly, then the labour cost is the amount that would have to be paid to the extra staff (i.e. the cash that would have to be sacrificed).

The relevant costs can also be called 'incremental costs'. That is, what matters is how the costs would change if the extra project were done.

Sunk and committed costs

Bygones are forever bygones. Sunk costs are always irrelevant for decisions. Sunk or committed costs can be treated interchangeably because an *irreversible* decision will have been made. This is an important issue in the context of capital investment appraisal (an aspect of finance, not covered in this book) because, once a decision is made to go ahead with a project, there are sunk and/or committed costs and these are, in effect, irrelevant costs.

Fixed costs

In most businesses, there are costs that are *fixed* (at least in the short-term) irrespective of how much business is done. These costs do not change with changes in the level of activity. For example, if a firm were to rent a building for its manufacturing facility, the rent would be the same regardless of the level of manufacturing activity taking place inside the building. This contrasts with costs that *vary* with the volume of business.

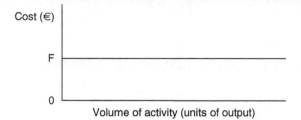

Cost (€)

F

0

Volume of activity (units of output)

12. Graph of fixed costs against the level of activity

Figure 12 shows a graph with fixed costs remaining constant, despite an increase in volume of activity. As the level of output increases, the fixed costs stay the same (at the amount OF).

Typically, fixed costs include rent, insurance, and cleaning costs and this would apply to a range of service industries such as banks, hotels, and supermarkets. Even some parts of labour costs in manufacturing companies are fixed in the short-term.

Treating a cost as fixed does *not* mean that it will be fixed forever. What the term *fixed* implies is that it is reasonable to treat such costs as unchanging irrespective of the volume of activity *for the period of activity under consideration.* Another way of expressing this concept is that certain costs can be treated as fixed *within the relevant range.* This means that, as long as activity does not go outside a particular range, these costs can be assumed to remain fixed. In the longer term, it is difficult to see any costs as being permanently fixed. For example, a company could rent out part of its building as business activity fell, thus reducing what was previously thought of as a fixed cost.

Step 'fixed' costs

Now consider the situation where there is a massive increase in business, for example because the firm has engaged in very substantial expansion overseas. If this happened, it would be necessary to open new offices, so that rental costs would no longer

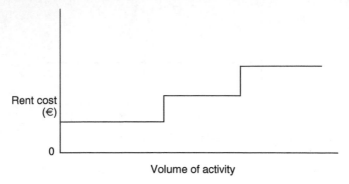

Rent cost
(€)

0

Volume of activity

13. Graph of rent cost against the level of activity

remain fixed. If this were the case, then the rental cost would behave as shown in Figure 13. Such cost behaviour is described as being 'step fixed'.

As the volume of activity increases from zero, the rent (a fixed cost) is unaffected. However, at a particular point, the volume of activity cannot increase without additional space being rented. The cost of renting the additional space will cause a 'step' in the rent cost. The higher rent cost will continue unaffected if volume were to rise further, until eventually another step point would be reached.

Variable costs

Variable costs are defined as those which vary with the volume of activity. In a manufacturing context, if a firm has no activity, it will incur no variable costs. For example, the use of raw materials might be zero if production is zero. Labour costs are also used as an example of variable costs, and this might apply in factories in some countries. Variable costs can also be called 'marginal costs'. In practice, many people now work in organizations in which labour costs do not vary with output, at least in the short-term.

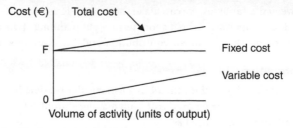

14. Graph of total cost against level of activity

Total costs

Figure 14 shows an example of total costs, including fixed and
variable. At zero activity, the variable costs are zero, so total cost
equals fixed cost. As activity increases, so variable cost increases
and therefore total cost does.

Break-even analysis

The above ideas about cost can be used to make decisions. The
first example is a decision about the scale of operations of an
entity, using break-even analysis. For this, the four key concepts in
Box 15 are needed.

Box 15
1. Fixed costs (in total).
2. Variable costs in total, and per unit of production.
3. Sales (i.e. the total sales figure in money terms), and the
   selling price per unit.
4. Output (volume).

Changing any one of these four will have an impact on the profit
of the business. If we increase the fixed costs of the firm, profit will
decline; if we increase the selling price, the profit will go up
(assuming that customers buy as many units, which is an issue of
economics rather than accounting). So, by looking at the relationships

between the variables, we can make short-term decisions.
Break-even analysis is about short-term profit planning. Two new
terms need to be explained: 'contribution' and 'break-even point'.

Contribution

The 'contribution' is the amount that a particular product line
helps towards covering fixed costs and making a profit. The
contribution is measured as:

$$\text{Sales} - \text{Variable costs}$$

This can also be calculated per unit of production. The
contribution per unit (CPU) is:

$$\text{CPU} = \text{Selling price per unit} - \text{Variable cost per unit}$$

That is, taking the selling price for one unit of production, and
then deducting all the variable costs for that one unit of
production, gives the contribution per unit.

Break-even point (BEP)

The break-even point is the volume of production at which the
firm makes zero profit. Therefore, the break-even point is the level at
which all costs (including fixed costs) can be paid for. The formula is:

$$\text{BEP} = \frac{\text{Total fixed costs}}{\text{Contribution per unit (CPU)}}$$

So, above the break-even point, any extra items sold will generate
profit. Every unit that is produced and sold in excess of the
break-even point will generate profit of the amount of the CPU.
The total profit made is:

$$\text{Units in excess of break-even point} \times \text{CPU}$$

If the firm does not reach break-even point, this implies that it has
not yet covered fixed costs and will therefore make a loss. The size

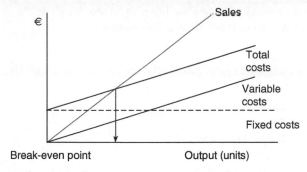

15. Break-even graph

of the loss will be the number of units under the break-even point, multiplied by the CPU.

The break-even point can be derived using the formula given above, or by drawing up a chart such as Figure 15.

Extra fixed costs

If extra fixed costs are incurred, as a result of an advertising campaign for example, the number of additional units to break even can be calculated as follows:

$$\frac{\text{Extra fixed costs}}{\text{CPU}}$$

For example, if a firm wants to place an advert in a magazine, it will want to know if the advert has been worthwhile. How many extra orders would the advert need to bring to justify the additional cost incurred by the advert? The answer is: the extra cost incurred divided by the CPU.

An example of break-even analysis: ToyCo

Let us now try an example of break-even analysis. ToyCo manufactures a popular children's toy. At present the

101

production is limited to a maximum of 50 toys per week. The management has the following information:

Unit selling price: €40
Unit variable costs:
    Materials €8
    Labour €10
Weekly expenses:
    Rent and rates €200
    Electricity €40
    Other fixed costs €68

The tasks are:

1. Calculate the break-even point.
2. If the company was aiming for a profit of €220 per week, how many toys would the company need to make and sell per week?
3. If output reached a maximum capacity, that is 50 toys per week, how much profit would the company make?
4. The company is then deciding whether to undertake an advertising campaign costing €100. How many toys would it need to sell in order to make the advertising worthwhile?

These tasks are achieved as follows:

1. *Calculate the break-even point using the formula*

Contribution per unit = unit selling price − unit variable costs

$$= €40 − €(8 + 10)$$

$$= €40 − €18$$

$$= €22 \text{ per unit}$$

$$\text{Break-even point} = \frac{\text{fixed costs}}{\text{CPU}}$$

$$= \frac{€200 + €40 + €68}{€22}$$

$$= \frac{€308}{€22}$$

$$= 14 \text{ units (toys)}$$

In summary, first we work out the contribution per unit for each toy; this is €22 per unit. Then we can use the CPU to work out the break-even point in units, which is 14 toys. The company therefore needs to make and sell 14 toys to cover its fixed costs; that is the point at which it makes zero profit. For every one unit that is then produced and sold after break-even point, the company will make €22 profit per item.

2. *If the company aims for a profit of €220 per week, how many toys must it make and sell per week in total?*

$$\text{Break-even point} = \frac{\text{Fixed costs} + \text{Desired profit}}{\text{Contribution per unit}}$$

$$= \frac{€308 + €220}{€22}$$

$$= 24 \text{ units (toys)}$$

Here, we have added the desired (target) profit to the fixed costs and divided by the CPU. We need 14 units to cover the fixed costs and another 10 units to make the desired profit. We could have divided the desired profit by CPU, i.e. €220/€22 = 10 units. Add these 10 units to the break-even amount: 10 + 14 = 24 units.

3. *If output reached maximum capacity, i.e. 50 toys per week, how much profit would the company make?*

If the number produced exceeds break-even point, then the profit is:

$$= \text{units in excess of break-even} \times \text{CPU}$$

$$= (50 - 14) \times €22$$

$$= 36 \times €22$$

$$= €792$$

The company's maximum output is 50 units. Assuming it makes and sells all 50 units, the company will exceed the break-even point by 36 units. It will make a profit on these 36 units with a CPU of €22 per item, i.e. €792 in all.

4. *The company has decided to undertake an advertising campaign costing €100. How many toys does it need to sell to make the advertising worthwhile?*

If extra fixed costs are incurred, in this case as a result of an advertising campaign, the number of additional units needed to break even is:

$$\frac{\text{Extra fixed costs}}{\text{CPU}}$$

$$= \frac{€100}{€22}$$

$$= 4.5 \text{ units}$$

$$= 5 \text{ toys (rounded up)}$$

As the entity can only make full units, the figure is rounded up to 5 units. The company therefore has to receive extra orders of 5 units or more for the advertising campaign to be worthwhile. This assumes that the company's full capacity would not be exceeded by this extra order.

Direct and indirect costs

Another way of looking at costs is that some are 'direct' (i.e. can be closely associated with a particular project) and others are 'indirect' or 'overhead' (i.e. relate to several projects or to the whole organization). Suppose that the project in question is the production of a car. Certain costs clearly relate to one particular car of the thousands being produced. Such costs include amounts of steel and labour. However, other costs relate to all the cars of the same type (e.g. the electricity to run the production line, or the salary of the supervisor of the production workers). Yet further costs relate to even wider operations (e.g. the expenses of running the head office of the company, which manufactures and sells many types of car).

Any costs that cannot be directly related to particular units of output are collected together in 'cost centres' (e.g. a production line or the head office) and then allocated down to a cost centre nearer to the level of the individual output. The head office costs get spread amongst the production lines; the production line costs get spread amongst the units produced on that line. Eventually, all the costs can be allocated to a particular unit of output. In a sense, then, the 'cost' of a particular car is a matter of opinion: it depends on how all the various overheads are allocated.

Activity-based costing

Sometimes, the above allocation methods seem arbitrary. Another approach, called activity-based costing (ABC), can be better. With ABC, the fundamental cost object is not a unit of product but an organizational activity, such as an event, task or unit of work. The costs of these activities are then used to allocate costs to products, customers, or services. This is shown in Figure 16 and in Box 16.

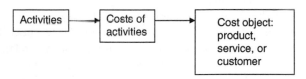

16. Outline of activity-based costing

Box 16

- Identify how products and/or services *drive* business activity.

- Define suitable cost pools for collecting together all the costs relating to these activities. These activity pools arise directly from the activities, which drive the costs. An example of such an activity is winning new customers.

- Collect all costs into activity pools.

- Calculate a cost driver rate for each activity cost pool. For example, these could be the cost per new customer order obtained.

- Allocate the costs in the activity cost pools to products according to the product's demand for the activity.

ABC aims to provide managers with an understanding about which overhead expenses vary with distinct cost drivers. It is more likely to be useful if direct labour is a small proportion of costs. It might be helpful when other ways of reporting costs have lost credibility with managers.

Pricing

Setting prices for products is an issue examined in micro-economics and marketing, but a few words should be said on the issue here. If a particular product is sold in a highly competitive market, the company may have little chance to influence the product's price. It is then vital to control costs, so that there is room for a profit to be made. In such circumstances, the accountants can help by using the techniques discussed above to establish a 'target cost'. If, instead, the product is highly specialized, the company might be involved in setting the price. In this case, the accountants can help by measuring the cost and then adding some percentage mark-up which enables a profit to be made by the whole company. This is called 'cost-plus pricing'.

Chapter 8
Accounting as control

Chapter 7 examined aspects of management accounting related to decision-making by managers. This chapter looks at some ways in which accounting can be used by managers to control their organizations. Among other things, the chapter addresses the following questions: How does budgeting work, and how is it useful? What are standard costs and how do they help in controlling production? How can a balanced scorecard improve control?

A budget and the budgeting process

A budget is a detailed document that sets out, in financial terms, the plans for income, expenditure, or cash movements in respect of a future period, for a unit of an organization or for the organization as a whole. There is also a budget for capital spending (e.g. on new buildings) but we do not deal with that here. All the individual budgets are part of an overall system to help to run the organization. Such a process can be just as useful for a government or a charity as it can be for a profit-seeking firm. In what follows, we use the latter as an example. An outline of the budgeting process is as seen in Box 17.

Box 17

1. Setting the aims and objectives of the firm.

2. Identifying the options available.

3. Evaluating the options and making decisions about them.

4. Making forecasts of income and expenses, based on these decisions.

5. Setting detailed plans or budgets.

6. Collecting information on what actually then happens, and exercising control.

There are two main high-level purposes of budgeting. The first is to optimize the use of the economic resources within the firm in order to maximize profit. The firm has limited economic resources available, so it needs to use them effectively in order to generate the maximum profit. The second purpose is to help the firm to achieve its overall strategic objectives. For example, the firm may decide to try to increase market share by 25 per cent, or it may want to reduce cost by 10 per cent. We will now look at six aspects of budgeting: planning, motivation, delegation, communication/coordination, control, and performance evaluation.

Planning

Firms need to plan ahead. By getting involved in the budgeting process, managers are forced to do this. Without the budgeting process, managers might just carry on with their routine tasks, and then engage in crisis management. By getting managers to think ahead, they foresee problems and are in a better position to prevent them arising.

Motivation

Budgets create targets for all levels of employees, and therefore provide something to aim for. The sales team will have sales targets to achieve by the end of the month or year, which may be linked to commission or bonuses. The production department will then have to produce so many of a particular item. The production department's cost-cutting efforts may also be linked to a bonus scheme. Providing people with a feasible target and perhaps a bonus scheme may help to generate positive behavioural patterns amongst staff. However, this is only likely if the targets are achievable and realistic, and if the staff have been involved in the budgeting process. This is one aspect of the 'behavioural problems' of budgeting, that account must be taken of the reactions of staff to the system.

Delegation

Budgets allow for responsibility to be passed down to lower levels of managers and staff by means of subsidiary budgets. The production director will know what the overall production aims are, allowing him or her to inform the relevant production managers who will then inform their relevant production supervisors. So, budgets allow for responsibility to be passed down the chain of command, even to the most junior employee. The previous paragraph pointed out that each level of employee should be involved, including pointing out if initial targets are impossible or unreasonable.

Communication/Coordination

Budgets facilitate better communication and coordination between departments and employees within the firm. Each manager creates a subsidiary budget, and these form the basis of the master budget. As all the managers (budget holders) have access to this master budget, they will understand the needs of their colleagues. All the subsidiary budgets are interrelated. The initial budget may be the sales budget. From this follows the production budget, then the material usage budget, and so on. So the production department will understand the needs of the sales department: the purchasing department will understand the needs of the production department, etc. Therefore budgeting will aid better communication and coordination between the different departments.

Control

Once a firm has created budgets, they can be used for control purposes. At the end of the respective accounting period, the firm can compare what actually happened with the estimated income and expenditure. Firms tend to do this at the end of every month. At this point, the management accountant sends the actual monthly figures, with the budgeted figures for comparison. Any differences between budgeted and actual figures are called variances and this method of comparison is called 'variance analysis', which is discussed further below for particular products. Managers need to investigate the differences (variances) and to identify the causes. These might include the original estimates being poorly thought out and incorrectly calculated; or possible overspending on materials.

Once the firm has determined the reasons behind the variances, it is in a better position to do something about such differences, that is, take corrective action. As noted above, there are various aspects of staff behaviour that should be considered. For example, if any unspent part of a travel cost budget is taken away at the end of each year, staff will be tempted to make unnecessary journeys near the end of the year because they like travel or because they fear that next year's budget will be reduced if the present one is underspent.

Performance evaluation

Budgets are a useful tool for measuring the performance of staff. A firm can use budgets to see how well, for example, the sales team is meeting its targets. The firm can compare actual results with budgeted figures to see how well staff are performing in their jobs. This may then be used for staff evaluations to determine who gets promotion. However, it is important to remember that many features of performance cannot be easily measured in monetary terms. A firm can use a series of 'key performance indicators'

(KPIs) to assess the performance of staff members and of the whole organization. Some of the KPIs are not financial, as explained in the last section of this chapter.

Constructing a cash flow forecast and budget

Let us take the simple but vital example of cash budgeting. This can only be done properly after all the other budgets have been drafted, because nearly all activities will affect cash. As usual, the management accountant must start with a forecast, then move towards a plan (a budget). The time frame for cash forecasts tends to be one year, broken down into twelve one-month periods. However, some businesses draw up cash forecasts extending to several years. There are three sections in a cash forecast:

Top section: Cash inflows/receipts
Middle section: Cash outflows/payments
Bottom section: End-of-period balances

Let us look at these in more detail.

Top section

Typical cash inflows include: cash sales, cash received from credit sales, new share capital, and loans. Sales can be on a cash basis or on a credit basis, as examined in Chapter 3. Cash from the first type will be received immediately, whereas cash from credit sales will come in over a period. For example, cash from credit sales made in January may be received in February, and so on. If credit terms are 30 days, we might assume that all credit sales will be received on time. However, in practice, some cash from credit sales may come in early, while other parts arrive after 60 days, 90 days or even more. Of course, account must also be taken of customers who might never pay. Once the detailed cash inflows for each month have been estimated, they can be added together to give the Total Cash Inflows.

Middle section

This section deals with all the cash outflows (payments). Typical cash outflows include see Box 18.

Again, it is vital to estimate the timing of any cash outflows. If a supplier has given the firm 30 days' credit to pay, this must be reflected in the cash flow forecast. If the firm receives goods in January and has 30 days' credit, it is likely to use the credit facility and pay the supplier in February. Once the detailed cash outflows have been estimated, they can be added up for each month to give the total cash outflows. This allows the calculation of the net cash inflow:

$$\text{Net cash inflow} = \text{Cash inflows} - \text{Cash outflows}$$

Bottom section

The last section of the cash flow budget deals with all the balances. The first line is the opening cash balance for each month. For new firms, the opening balance will be zero. For continuing firms, the previous month's closing cash balance is bought forward, i.e. the previous month's closing balance is this month's opening balance. Here is an example of the bottom section, with an explanation, below:

	January	February	March
Opening balance	0	400	−200
Net cash inflow	400	−600	350
Closing balance	400	−200	150

January: Opening balance of €0 plus net cash inflow of €400 equals the closing balance for that month, €400. The closing balance of January is the opening balance for February.

February: Opening balance of €400 plus net cash inflow of minus €600 equals closing balance of minus €200. The closing balance of February is the opening balance for March.

March: Opening balance of minus €200 plus net cash inflow of €350 equals closing balance of €150.

However, let's look again at the balance at the end of February. What does this imply?

A negative cash balance is, of course, impossible unless the business is allowed to go into a negative balance at the bank, but that might be expensive. The management accountants should notice this problem with the forecast, and take steps to slow down payments, speed up receipts, or arrange low-cost loans. They will then adjust the forecast, and make it a 'budget'.

Flexible budgeting and zero-base budgeting

Given that the budgets are all connected to each other, any one budget can be out-dated by events elsewhere in the firm. Let us consider the cash budget or the budget for the use of materials, which had been prepared on a monthly basis for the year ahead. Suppose that production and sales are much higher than expected in the first month of the year, and that this seems likely to continue. It would then make little sense to assess the materials used, or the cash coming in and out, as though the originally-planned volumes had happened. The budgets need to be able to expand and contract, so that managers throughout the firm can be fairly assessed. This is achieved through 'flexible budgets'.

When establishing a budget for a period, the quickest and easiest approach is to start with the previous period's budget, adjusting it for expected inflation and any major expected changes. However, if an organization carries on doing that for many years, it might forget to ask whether particular activities are really needed or whether certain activities could be done more cheaply or done completely differently. Consequently, there is a good argument for demanding that managers should start from scratch each year, with 'zero-base budgeting'.

Standard costing

This idea of budgets can be applied at a detailed level to the production of a particular type of good. This can involve calculating a 'standard cost'. To do this, the management accountant looks at past, present, and future costs. The management accountant will talk to the purchasing department and attempt to foresee any future price rises of raw materials and so on. The purchasing department will have better knowledge of what the firm's suppliers are doing. The management accountant will also consult the personnel department to see if there are any likely future rises in labour pay rates.

The aim of the exercise is to foresee changes in costs and build them into the budgeting process. That way, if costs do change, at least the system of control will be more precise. There are several levels of standards that can be used by the accountant. One is called the 'ideal standard' and another is the 'attainable standard'.

Ideal and attainable standards

The ideal standard assumes that the operations will work at maximum efficiency, that there will be no wastage, no strikes, no shortages of inventory, and so on. There is therefore no allowance for any problem. Actually operating at maximum level, however, is very unlikely. In practice, suppliers may let the firm down; staff may not turn up to work; etc. So the next level of standard takes these issues into account. This attainable standard bases costs on what the firm can realistically achieve. The accountant will provide for certain allowances, such as machine break downs and delivery hold-ups.

Common items for which to calculate standard costs

There are three common types of items for which standard costs are established: materials, labour, and overheads. Let us take the example of materials. Suppose that, for a particular manufacturing job, the production department expects to use 5 kilograms of material, which should cost €4.50 per kilogram. Also, the accountant discovers that each product requires 4 hours of unskilled labour, payable at €6 per hour. These are then the standard costs from which to derive the budgets and then to see whether the actual production meets the standard. This comparison is called variance analysis.

In variance analysis, we compare actual data with budgeted data (the standard costs). Variance analysis is the process of breaking down any variances into their component parts for detailed investigation. Variance analysis is a technique used for controlling costs. When comparing the standard cost of materials with the data on actual usage, there are two types of material variances that can be identified: material price variance and material usage variance.

The material price variance is the difference between what the firm actually paid for materials and what it should have paid (according to the standard price as predicted by the management accountant). This variance is calculated as:

$$(\text{Actual price} - \text{Standard price}) \times \text{Actual quantity}$$

The material usage variance is the difference between the quantity actually used and what should have been used. This is:

$$(\text{Actual quantity} - \text{Standard quantity}) \times \text{Standard price}$$

Overall, we have:

$$\text{Total material variance} = \text{Actual material costs} - \text{Standard material costs}$$

$$= (\text{Actual price} \times \text{Actual quantity}) - (\text{Standard price} \times \text{Standard quantity})$$

$$= \text{Material price variance} + \text{Material usage variance}$$

Numerical example

Suppose that a company uses a particular material which has the following established standard costs: Standard price = €12 per kg, and Standard usage = 24 kg.

In practice, the following occur: Actual price = €10 per kg, and Actual usage = 28 kg.

Let us now calculate: (a) material price variance; (b) material usage variance; and (c) total material variance.

$$\text{The Material price variance} = (\text{Actual price} - \text{Standard price}) \times \text{Actual quantity}$$

$$= (€10 - €12) \times 28$$

$$= €2 \times 28$$

$$= €56 \text{ (F)}$$

It is not normal to use minus signs in variance analysis because some *reductions* are good. Once the accountants have calculated the variance, they need to consider whether the variance is favourable (F) to the firm, or unfavourable (U). Some companies use the word 'adverse' (A) instead of unfavourable. In the above case, the company paid less than it had expected for materials, so the variance is favourable.

The Material usage variance = (Actual quantity − Standard quantity)
$$\times \text{Standard price}$$

$$= (28 \text{ kg} - 24 \text{ kg}) \times €12 \text{ per kg}$$

$$= 4 \times €12$$

$$= €48 \text{ (U)}$$

In order to express the variance as a monetary figure, the accountants multiply by the standard price. If the figures in brackets are already expressed in money terms then they multiply by the actual quantity (see the material price variance).

The Total material variance = Actual material costs
$$- \text{Standard material costs}$$

$$= (\text{Actual price} \times \text{Actual quantity}) \text{ less}$$
$$(\text{Standard price} \times \text{Standard quantity})$$

$$= (€10 \times 28) - (€12 \times 24)$$

$$= €280 - €288$$

$$= €8 \text{ (F)}$$

Check:

Material price + Material usage

$$= €56 \text{ (F)} - €48 \text{ (U)}$$

$$= €8 \text{ (F)}$$

The company was €56 better off in terms of price, yet €48 worse off in terms of usage. So the overall net effect is €8 better off than standard.

We could now explain the overall material variance. Why was the company €8 better off than expected? Looking at the original data, we see that the company paid €2 less than expected for each kilogram of material, which may imply that it used cheaper materials to do the job. In terms of usage, it should have consumed 24 kilograms but ended up using 28 kilograms. Because it used a cheaper material it may have had more waste, thus explaining why more material was used. However, the advantage of the cheaper price outweighed the disadvantage of the amount of material used.

Why did the firm end up using cheaper material? Was it because this was the only material available at the time? This is something to look into, which will perhaps enable management to plan ahead. The same approach can be taken to the labour costs and the overhead costs.

A balanced scorecard

Earlier, there was mention of the idea of key performance indicators, some of which are non-financial. A particular version of this approach to planning, called the 'balanced scorecard', involves three additional perspectives: keeping customers happy, having good internal processes/objectives, and achieving learning/growth. These perspectives are assessed by a mixture of financial and other measures, such as number of injuries in the factory or amount of greenhouse gas emissions. The process identifies the critical success factors which must be achieved in each period in order to reach long-term strategic goals. Figure 17 gives an example of using the balanced scorecard.

Balanced Scorecard Perspective	10 Market Forces (Objective)	GRI Measure: How success or failure is measured using the triple bottom line (a common framework for sustainability reporting)	Target: The level of performance or rate of improvement required
Financial	'Green' consumers	Energy consumption footprint (annualized lifetime energy requirements) of major products	Annual reduction in energy footprint for new products
Financial	Energy crunch	Direct energy use segmented by source	100% renewal energy
Financial	Financial	Increase/decrease in retained earnings at end of period	Percentage
Internal	Pollution and health	Standard injury, lost day, and absentee rates and number of work-related fatalities (including subcontractors)	0 lost-time injuries & fatalities, or long-term illnesses
Internal	Climate change	Total greenhouse gas emissions	Annualized reduction
Internal	Governments and regulators	Incidents and fines for non-compliance with all laws and regulations	0 incidents or fines
People and Knowledge	Civil society/NGOs	Policies, guidelines, and procedures to address needs of indigenous people	Number of indigenous employees
People and Knowledge	Activist shareholders	Business units currently operating or planning operations in or around protected or sensitive areas	Number of employees trained in environmental management practices
Customer	Erosion of trust/transparency	Policy to exclude all child labour	No child labour
Customer	Globalization backlash	Supplier performance related to environmental commitments	Use of 100% organic cotton or coffee

17. **Using the four perspectives of the balanced scorecard**

Epilogue

Each chapter of this book opens with some questions addressed in the chapter. We can now take an overview of the whole of accounting, and look at some high level questions.

So, just how important has accounting been in the history of the world?

For readers of this book who have started reading here, the above question will seem outrageously overblown and self-serving, especially coming from an author who is a qualified accountant, a professor of accounting, and a former co-writer of accounting standards. However, readers who began at the beginning will remember that research suggests that the need to keep accounts was associated with the development of numbers and writing. Further, all the good (and bad) things that come from government rest on taxation, which rests on accounting.

It is, of course, possible to claim too much. In the nineteenth century, several writers claimed that the invention of double-entry bookkeeping (DEB) led to the rise of capitalism. However, there are many problems with this idea: (i) an owner's interest can be recorded and profit can be calculated without DEB; (ii) until the nineteenth century, annual profit was seldom calculated by those who used DEB; and (iii) most of the vital questions for an entrepreneur (e.g. those of Chapters 7 and 8) are not the focus of DEB.

Nevertheless, it is clear that some sophisticated record-keeping system is necessary for larger and complex international organizations. DEB serves well in this function, which is why it has gradually replaced other systems around the world. Furthermore, its outputs can be used to inform the providers of external finance, and in practice DEB has survived all alternatives, perhaps because it is the fittest.

How exact a science is accounting?

If the above question had been set in an exam at a respectable university, one hopes that candidates would tear into it with gusto, first doubting that accounting is a science at all. DEB might well be called a craft, but one remembers that the civilized world is kept afloat by crafts such as plumbing or shoe-making. The use of the information from DEB is perhaps a series of technologies or technical arts: financial reporting and management accounting. These arts involve a great deal of judgement. Even a nice solid asset such as an office building has a potential plethora of 'values': historical cost, depreciated historical cost, current replacement cost, net realizable value, discounted expected net cash inflows, and others. Accountants use different numbers for different purposes, and this has varied by country. A balance sheet contains lots of numbers which have been measured differently but are nevertheless added together. Profit is calculated by combining some rather definite numbers (e.g. sales and wages) with some difficult estimates (e.g. pension expenses), some gains which are not expected in cash for the foreseeable future (e.g. rises in value of investment properties) and some wild guesses (e.g. impairments of goodwill).

If we are outsiders, can we rely on accounting?

Given the answer to the previous question, outsiders (e.g. bankers or shareholders) clearly need to be wary. The published financial statements rely on many estimates, and they are, in a sense, marketing documents: the company wants your money. History is replete with spectacular examples of bad reporting. Nevertheless, things have improved. There are now fairly detailed rules on what to disclose and how to measure. Monitoring and enforcement have been strengthened around the world, especially in this millennium. In some countries at least, directors can be locked up for bad accounting, and auditors are properly frightened of litigation and of regulators. There are probably more examples of the market not properly absorbing published information (e.g. the continuous losses of General Motors up to its collapse in 2008) as there are examples of wholly misleading accounting (e.g. Enron in 2001).

Did accounting cause the global financial crisis?

The simple answer to this question is: no. Too many people borrowed too much money. In some cases, the money was spent on assets which the buyers did understand (e.g. houses in Spain). In other cases, the buyers did not understand (e.g. various derivatives in the USA). Irrational exuberance eventually leads to a crash.

Some accuse accounting of using too much 'fair value' (current market prices), but it is difficult to see how the market would operate better by reporting out-of-date numbers. Of course, reporting the falls in market value of assets which are not going to be sold needs to be separated from more definite losses. When it comes to the valuation of longer-term receivables, there is an argument for attempting to foresee lifetime losses rather than only accounting for losses when they happen. As I write (in 2013) the standard-setters are still grappling with that problem.

So, is financial reporting nearly as good as it can get?

In an international context, the differences have been greatly reduced in the last decade. This helps French investors to assess US companies, or UK multinationals to assess or to consolidate Brazilian subsidiaries.

Improvements are still needed. The standard-setters cannot explain why there are two income statements (profit/loss and other comprehensive income). Most leases are still (in 2014) not recognized as liabilities. Reporting by insurance companies is almost unregulated after decades of drafting the rules.

Can we trust the auditors? *Quis custodiet ipsos custodes?*

There are certainly some worrying things about audit. Let us take the context of UK listed companies. In practice, an audit firm is largely selected by a company's chief financial officer, who is usually a former auditor, sometimes from the audit firm selected. An auditor generally refers to the company as the 'client' although the auditor is supposed to be working for the company's shareholders. The auditor often does non-audit work for the 'client', whom it would therefore not wish to upset. Then, there is the problem that an audit firm can remain in place for decades. When a large listed company does change its auditor, it swaps from one Big-4 firm to another: the Big-4 audit nearly all the top 100 (and even the top 250) companies. It is not surprising that, when companies fail, there is anger in the question: where were the auditors?

However, some progress has been made. The types of non-audit work allowed for auditors have been restricted; disclosures of fees paid to auditors have been required; the partner in charge of the audit is rotated even if the audit firm is not; the firms require partners to produce annual evidence of 'professional scepticism';

increasingly strict independence rules are enforced; and the regulators have become more intrusive.

The dominance of the Big-4 is not surprising. The firms need to be big in order to operate throughout the world because their clients do. There has to be a massive investment in training and technology. Big listed companies cannot risk signalling anything less than top quality audit, so they feel that they must use the Big-4. However, the dominance is alarming. It does look anti-competitive. There is also the practical problem that, on many big deals (e.g. a take-over battle), all four firms are involved in some capacity, so top-level independent advice is hard to find. It is clear that the US and EU regulators should not have allowed the former Big-8 to become the Big-5 as a result of mergers. This was followed by the demise of Andersen following the collapse of its client, Enron, in 2001. These events shocked the remaining Big-4 into many improvements and led to increases in controls on auditors. However, one wonders whether the regulators now have to tread carefully: could they allow (or push) another audit firm to fail so that we have then to manage with only a Big-3?

Can the managers rely on their own accounting?

Managers may be less likely to mislead themselves than to mislead outsiders, but one manager may be tempted to mislead another. On the whole, though, the problems of management accounting are about poor design. If the management accounting system measures the wrong thing, the manager's efforts will be misdirected. By analogy, if the banker is rewarded according to the total amount lent, the banker will lend to people irrespective of whether they will repay. The most famous book on the history of management accounting is entitled *Relevance Lost*, in which the authors complain that management accounting has not changed much since the 1920s and is suited more to smoke-stack industries than to the modern high-tech, fast-changing world.

Many problems with budgetary control relate to perverse incentives: 'I must spend this year's budget for travel, otherwise next year's might be reduced'. However, these problems are increasingly well understood. Management accounting in any particular firm can be designed without the constraints of old laws and standards, even though it might struggle to escape old ideas.

Further reading

Chapter 2: The international evolution of accounting

A History of Financial Accounting by J. R. Edwards (Routledge, 1989).

Double Entry: How the Merchants of Venice Shaped the Modern World—and How their Invention Could Make or Break the Planet by Jane Gleeson-White (Allen and Unwin, 2011).

Chapter 3: The fundamentals of financial accounting
Chapter 4: Financial reports of listed companies

Financial Accounting and Reporting: A Global Perspective by M. Lebas, H. Stolowy, and Y. Ding (Cengage Learning, 2013).

Financial Accounting: An International Introduction by D. Alexander and C. Nobes (Prentice Hall, 2013).

Company Valuation under IFRS by N. Antill and K. Lee (Harriman House, 2008).

Chapter 5: International differences and standardization

Comparative International Accounting by C. Nobes and R. H. Parker (Prentice Hall, 2012).

Financial Reporting and Global Capital Markets: A History of the International Accounting Standards Committee, 1973-2000 by K. Camfferman and S. A. Zeff (Oxford University Press, 2007).

The Economics and Politics of Accounting: International Perspectives on Research Trends, Policy and Practice by C. Leuz, D. Pfaff, and A. Hopwood (Oxford University Press, 2004).

Chapter 6: Regulation and audit

Contemporary Issues in Accounting Regulation by S. McLeay and
    A. Riccaboni (Kluwer, 2001).
The Audit Society: Rituals of Verification by Michael Power (Oxford
    University Press, 1999).

Chapter 7: Internal decision-making
Chapter 8: Accounting as control

Introduction to Management Accounting by A. Bhimani, C. T. Horngren,
    G. L. Sundem, W. O. Stratton, D. Burgstahler, and J. Schatzberg
    (Pearson, 2012).
Relevance Lost: The Rise and Fall of Management Accounting by
    H. T. Johnson and R. S. Kaplan (Harvard Business School Press,
    1991).

Further reading

Glossary of key terms

This Glossary is primarily written in English as used by the International Accounting Standards Board (IASB). Much of this is British English, although there are cross-references to US English.

accounting policies
The detailed methods of presentation, recognition, and measurement that a particular company has chosen from those generally accepted by law, accounting standards or commercial practice.

accounting standards
Technical accounting rules of financial reporting, as set by private-sector committees.

accrual basis of accounting
The practice of concentrating on the period to which an expense or income relates rather than on the period in which cash is paid or received. The accrual basis is used for all the financial statements except the cash flow statement.

activity-based costing (ABC)
The practice of relating as many expenses as possible, often previously regarded as overheads, to particular production activities.

asset
According to the IASB: a resource controlled by an entity, as a result of past events, from which future economic benefits are expected to flow to the entity. It is not necessary for the entity to own the asset.

balance sheet

A snapshot of the accounting records of assets, liabilities, and equity of a business at a particular moment, most obviously the accounting year end. The IASB has adopted the term 'statement of financial position' instead.

budgetary control

A process by which financial control is exercised over an entity by establishing a detailed, monetarily quantified plan for parts of the enterprise, and then reviewing and adjusting activities in the light of subsequent performance compared to the plan.

comprehensive income

All the income and expenses recorded for a period, not just those recorded in profit or loss.

creative accounting

The stretching of the rules of financial reporting in order to present a better picture of an entity.

credit

In the context of bookkeeping, one of the two types of entry, denoting in this case an increase in liabilities, equity, or income, or a decrease in assets or expenses.

current assets and liabilities

Items on a balance sheet that are not intended for continuing use in the business, or that are expected to be received or paid in cash within one year.

debit

In the context of bookkeeping, one of the two types of entry, denoting in this case increases in assets or expenses, or decreases in liabilities, equity, or income.

earnings

A technical accounting term, meaning the amount of profit available to the ordinary shareholders (UK)/common stockholders (US). That is, it is the profit or loss after all operating expenses, interest, taxes and dividends on preference shares. 'Earnings' does not include other comprehensive income.

fair value

The price at which an asset could be sold or a liability settled in a market.

FIFO (first-in, first-out)
An assumption (for accounting purposes) that the first units to be received as part of inventories are the first ones to be used up or sold. This means that the most recent units are deemed to be those left at the period end.

finance lease
A contract that transfers substantially all of the risks and rewards of an asset to the lessee.

goodwill
The amount paid for a company in excess of the fair value of its net assets at the date of acquisition.

impairment
The loss of value of an asset due to unexpected events.

liabilities
Present obligations of an entity, arising from past events, the settlement of which is expected to result in an outflow of resources (usually cash). They include provisions.

LIFO (last-in, first-out)
An assumption (for accounting purposes only) that the most recent units to be received as part of inventories are the first ones to be used up or sold. This means that the oldest units are deemed to be those left at the period end.

net realizable value (NRV)
The amount that could be raised by selling an asset, less the costs of the sale and any costs to bring the asset into a saleable state.

off-balance sheet finance
An entity's obligations that are not recorded on its balance sheet. One important example of off-balance sheet finance is the existence of any leases (operating leases) that are not treated as assets and liabilities.

other comprehensive income (OCI)
Various gains and losses excluded from profit or loss. Examples include gains on revaluing certain assets.

overhead costs
Expenses of a business that cannot be traced to units of production or to processes that produce particular single products.

provision
A liability of uncertain timing or amount. However, the word is also used in the UK to mean an allowance against the value of an asset. Contrast this to reserve.

recoverable amount
The higher of an asset's discounted cash flows and net selling price. This amount is used as the measure of an impaired asset under IFRS.

reserves
UK or IFRS term for undistributed gains. These include accumulated profits and revaluations. There is no equivalent US term. Reserves should be distinguished from provisions. Reserves belong to shareholders and are part of a total of shareholders' equity, which also includes share capital. US accountants and others talk about a 'bad debt reserve' (meaning impairment) or 'pension reserve' (meaning provision).

true and fair view
The overriding legal requirement for the presentation of financial statements of companies in the United Kingdom, most of the (British) Commonwealth and the European Union. The nearest IFRS or US equivalent is 'fair presentation'.

window dressing
The manipulation of figures in financial statements in order to make them appear better (or perhaps worse) than they otherwise would be.

zero-base budgeting
A system of budgetary control which involves a starting from scratch each year.

Index

Index

LEADERSHIP
A Very Short Introduction
Keith Grint

In this *Very Short Introduction* Keith Grint prompts the reader to rethink their understanding of what leadership is. He examines the way leadership has evolved from its earliest manifestations in ancient societies, highlighting the beginnings of leadership writings through Plato, Sun Tzu, Machiavelli and others, to consider the role of the social, economic, and political context undermining particular modes of leadership. Exploring the idea that leaders cannot exist without followers, and recognising that we all have diverse experiences and assumptions of leadership, Grint looks at the practice of management, its history, future, and influence on all aspects of society.

www.oup.com/vsi

ONLINE CATALOGUE
A Very Short Introduction

Our online catalogue is designed to make it easy to find your ideal Very Short Introduction. View the entire collection by subject area, watch author videos, read sample chapters, and download reading guides.

http://fds.oup.com/www.oup.co.uk/general/vsi/index.html

SOCIAL MEDIA
Very Short Introduction

Join our community

www.oup.com/vsi

- Join us online at the official Very Short Introductions **Facebook** page.
- Access the thoughts and musings of our authors with our online **blog**.
- Sign up for our monthly **e-newsletter** to receive information on all new titles publishing that month.
- Browse the full range of Very Short Introductions online.
- Read **extracts** from the Introductions for free.
- Visit our library of **Reading Guides**. These guides, written by our expert authors will help you to question again, why you think what you think.
- If you are a teacher or lecturer you can order inspection copies quickly and simply via our website.